WINNING THE ASHES DOWN UNDER

The Captain's Story

Andrew Strauss

with Simon Hughes

HODDER

First published in Great Britain in 2011 by Hodder & Stoughton
An Hachette UK company
First published in paperback in 2011

1

A CIP catalogue record for this title is available from the British Library

Paperback ISBN 978 1 444 73621 2
Ebook ISBN 978 1 444 73622 9

Typeset in Minon Pro by Hewer Text UK, Ltd, Edinburgh

Printed and bound by CPI Group (UK) Ltd, Croydon, CR0 4YY

Hodder & Stoughton policy is to use papers that are natural, renewable
and recyclable products and made from wood grown in sustainable
forests. The logging and manufacturing processes are expected to
conform to the environmental regulations of the country of origin.

Hodder & Stoughton Ltd
338 Euston Road
London NW1 3BH

www.hodder.co.uk

WINNING THE ASHES DOWN UNDER

The Captain's Story

For Ruth, Sam and Luca

CONTENTS

ACKNOWLEDGEMENTS

THERE is clearly a huge amount of work that goes into putting a book together. It is fair to say that much of my time over the last six months has been taken up on the cricket field, and so much of the burden has fallen on the shoulders of others. I would like to take this opportunity to thank Simon Hughes, in particular, for your great ability to question, probe, cajole and ultimately to squeeze every last bit of information about the Ashes out of me. You have been a pleasure to work with.

I would also like to thank Roddy Bloomfield, Sarah Hammond and everyone at Hodder and Stoughton, who have waited patiently for the manuscript to be produced. It is fantastic to be involved with such a great publisher.

It would be remiss of me not to thank Andy Flower, all the management of the England Cricket team, and of course all the players who took part during the Ashes of 2010–11. Without you guys there would be very little interest in a book like this.

Finally, and most importantly I would like to thank Ruth, my wife, and Sam and Luca, my boys, for putting up with me being away from home for so long over the winter, and always brightening up my day when I am at home.

Simon Hughes would like to thank the faithful transcribers and Tim Waller, the immaculate copyeditor, who translated his convoluted interviews with Andrew Strauss into something more coherent.

Photographic Acknowledgements
AFP/Getty Images; Scott Barbour/Getty Images; Hamish Blair/Getty Images; Mark Dadswell/Getty Images; Stu Forster/ Getty Images; Julian Herbert/Getty Images; Paul Kane/Getty Images; Morne de Klerk/Getty Images; Mark Nolan/ Getty Images; Steve Parsons/PA Wire/Press Association Images; Ryan Pierse/Getty Images; Quinn Rooney/Getty Images; Clive Rose/Getty Images; Tom Shaw/Getty Images; Cameron Spencer/Getty Images; Bob Thomas/Popperfoto/ Getty Images; William West/AFP/Getty Images; Krystle Wright/AFP/Getty Images.

1

THE HOLY GRAIL

29 December 2010, Melbourne

IT is just after 3 p.m. on the fourth day of the Melbourne Test. We are sitting in the cavernous MCG dressing rooms – Aussie Rules teams use them to warm up in, so there are kicking nets everywhere. We have won the Ashes! And we've done it in Australia – for the first time in a generation! Make that two generations. Twenty-four years of hurt.

Paul Collingwood, Kevin Pietersen, Ian Bell, Alastair Cook and I have been chatting about the differences from the Melbourne Test four years ago. The contrast couldn't be greater. Back then, the Ashes had already been sacrificed and we'd been humiliated at the MCG. We'd batted first on Boxing Day and been bowled out very cheaply – I was Shane Warne's 700th Test wicket. Australia got 419 and we were bowled out cheaply again. We lost by an innings in three days. Afterwards, we sat in those enormous dressing rooms, feeling terrible.

Now here we are, in the same spot, with completely contrasting emotions. We have beaten Australia by an innings, for the second time in the series, and retained the Ashes. We've come such a long way in those four years. For me to be involved in the management side is really satisfying, but the way the players have developed is great testament to them and their willingness to push themselves after that chastening experience.

Having that context makes our celebrations all the more special, because the boot was so firmly on the other foot four years ago. We had to face the fact then that we were miles off the standard we needed to be, and it was embarrassing to realise that we were second-class citizens next to that Australian team. Not only that, but we were constantly being made to pay for it off the pitch, with Aussies coming up and telling us we were useless, and English supporters saying that we were a disgrace and should be ashamed to be putting on those Three Lions. For the likes of Collingwood and myself, it was certainly the lowest point in our careers. Even Pietersen, although he scored runs in that series, still had to endure all that stuff off the pitch.

This time, our families came to join the celebrations for a while, which was fantastic, and then they left us to it. I said a few words, Andy said a few words. I proposed toasts to the support staff, who do so much hard work and never get the praise. Then there were a couple of toasts to absent friends.

We all felt for Stuart Broad not being there, having played such an important part at the beginning of the tour and in our progress as a side over the eighteen months leading up to the Ashes. Graham Gooch had gone home for Christmas and we felt he deserved to be there as much as anyone for the sheer volume of work he had put in during the early part of the tour. Despite all he's achieved in the game, he's first at the ground every morning, throwing thousands of balls for the players, and he's a great example of someone who is willing to do the hard work for the team rather than just for himself. We missed him greatly.

What makes those times so special is the strength of the emotions. There were more toasts, then the guys moved from group to group, talking about what had gone on, reminiscing about moments that had stood out in the series. There was a real sense that we'd been through it all together. At no stage of the tour had there been cliques or anything like that, and certainly at this time of victory and celebration it was very special to have such a close-knit group of players. That moment as much as anything completely vindicated the decision to go on a team-bonding camp before the tour.

When we had turned up at the MCG that morning Australia were six down and still 246 behind. Harris wasn't expected to bat, so we knew we only needed three wickets. It was possibly the most frustrating session of cricket I have ever played. It was horrendous out there. In a situation like that, you can't help expecting it to happen – you're sure there's enough in the wicket to make it happen. But you have to control your emotions; you're so close to what you came for but you're not there yet.

Siddle was chancing his arm and frustrating us, and Haddin was proving difficult to remove. A few of our fielders were getting irritated with each other. Swann kept on almost getting them out, but the ball would just clear the ropes or go wide of the fielders. Fortunately, Siddle eventually slogged one to Pietersen running round from long-on, then Hilfenhaus inside-edged a ball from Bresnan and Matt Prior took a great catch down the leg side – and there was pandemonium.

There were so many emotions – joy, relief, satisfaction after all the hard work we'd put in – suddenly it had all been worthwhile. For those of us who had been there four years ago it was revenge, and for guys who had never played at the MCG before it was surely the finest Test match they'd ever experienced.

Above all, it was thoroughly deserved. That was the incredible thing, just looking at each other and saying, 'We've done it – we have done it. We've retained the Ashes.' There was no worrying about going on to win the series or anything like that. At that stage it was a matter of appreciating that we'd done something pretty amazing. It wasn't just the fact that we'd retained the Ashes, but the manner in which we'd won the two games. We'd been so utterly dominant.

There hadn't been much chance for me to say anything to the team straight after the game. There were high-fives and hugs for all the support staff, then just time for a couple of sips of beer before I headed out again for all the interviews, while the lads set off on a lap of the pitch. I finally joined them just as they were doing the Sprinkler Dance in front of the Barmy Army. I was worried that it might come across as being triumphant, but at that time it seemed the right thing to do, and the players certainly enjoyed it.

It was only after we'd completed the lap of the pitch and got back to the dressing rooms that it all sank in. For me those times after you've won something significant are the reason you play cricket. You talk about what's happened in the matches; you talk about the personal battles you've been having with yourselves as much as anything, the lack of sleep, feeling uncomfortable against a certain bowler – and suddenly it doesn't matter, because you've won.

KP came over and said, 'This is our best achievement ever on a cricket field. No one can ever take this away from us.' I looked at him and it was true. We'd won the Ashes Down Under – the holy grail. We'd found the holy grail after twenty-four years of searching. And this is how we did it.

2

STEPPING STONES

January 2009

THE situation when we got back from the 2008 tour of India was a bit of a train crash. On TV it was flashing up on Sky News that Kevin Pietersen had demanded that Peter Moores should go, and the ECB were deciding what course of action they were going to take.

Those of us who had been involved in India knew that something had to give – it had been pretty unworkable between Pietersen and Moores. They hadn't got on before Pietersen took over the captaincy. They just didn't see eye to eye on the way the England team should be run. Moores was very keen on pushing players all the time. He'd always be in your ear about doing more slip-catching, or improving one certain shot, or making sure you were measuring your hydration levels. KP, being the character he is, likes to be left to his own devices to play his own game. So there was conflict there from the start.

Once they were together as captain and coach there was a strong feeling in the team that it would be okay as long as England were winning, but as soon as we started losing, it was going to be tough for them to work together, and that's what happened in India. Their relationship was very fraught. They weren't really talking much to each other, and I think the players all felt that they were caught in the middle and being forced into one camp or another. It was horrible.

When Pietersen had been appointed, I was frustrated. Not so much because I hadn't been made captain, but because the selectors hadn't come up to me and said, 'Look, you're a strong candidate for the job, but we want one captain for all forms of the game.' I could definitely understand their reasons for it, but I was still a little dispirited at the thought that my chance might have passed. Obviously, I'd had opportunities to captain England prior to that, but it suddenly became very clear that they'd chosen to look beyond me. And that was fine – I wasn't going to make a big song and dance about it, but deep down I was thinking, 'I would love to have done that job.'

In India there had been some chat about how it would play out – is Moores going to stay on? Is KP going to stay on? I still had ambitions to do the job again, but at that stage I was beginning to think that there might be some sense in passing it on from our generation – the likes of me, Flintoff, Pietersen, Collingwood – and going straight to Cook or someone like that, so that they could refresh the team. Cook was very in tune with the younger players.

While the Pietersen and Moores story rumbled on, Hugh Morris, the England Cricket managing director, rang me and asked what my thoughts were on the whole situation. I said we should consider moving on to someone like Cook – by this time it had become pretty clear that KP wasn't going to keep his position. Morris said, 'That's fine, but would you be willing to do it if we offered it to you?' And I said I would.

Things were happening very fast, and I had to think about what it meant for our family. I wasn't playing one-day cricket at that stage, so did it mean I was going to come back in the one-day side? I'd seen how much the job had taken out of Nasser Hussain and Michael Vaughan, and so I had to get my head round the whole idea of the challenge that lay in front of me. Pretty soon afterwards, national selector Geoff Miller asked me to come to Lord's, and that was when I was actually offered the job.

Once we got the formalities out of the way I had the press conference. It was quite a nerve-wracking experience, because cricket was in the news for the wrong reasons: the Pietersen and Moores saga had put us on the front page of the papers. So facing me at Lord's were a huge number of journalists, firing questions that varied dramatically in nature – from the bog-standard cricketing stuff to 'How are you going to heal these wounds?', 'Which players are for who?' and 'Which players are against who?'

The real nitty-gritty had to start pretty quickly. We were leaving for the tour of the West Indies in eight or nine days, and I had to sit down with Andy Flower, who'd been appointed stand-in coach. He had quite deep reservations about whether he should be taking over in those circumstances. He was very close to Peter Moores, and he'd heard that Pietersen had wanted him out as well.

We went to see a conflict-resolution specialist in the City to talk about how to deal with the situation. The first thing we were told was that we had to gauge where the players were with this, so we needed to talk with them individually. So that's what I did. It became clear quite quickly that the players just wanted to move on and get behind something, and not be stuck in the middle. In any case, a lot of the problems had been solved now because the captain and coach who didn't get on were no longer there.

Another thing the specialist raised was the need to put together a code of values as a group. People talk about charters and so on, and I'd always been cynical about that sort of thing, but they said, 'Look, this is a great opportunity for you to turn over a new leaf for the side. How do you want to go about playing your cricket? What does it mean to play for England? How are you going to operate on this tour? Without some ideas that the players have some involvement in, you're always going to be banging your head against a brick wall.' So they helped us come up with a very rudimentary first draft of a charter with the players at the airport before we left.

One line was 'The team is not a lease car' – the idea being that a lease car is one that you just thrash and bump around and don't really care about. It's our own team and we need to treat it as such. The charter actually plays a very important part in our group now – it's not just a bit of laminated paper – and it's the discussions and the chat and the 'what ifs' that you go through that make it mean something.

3

STRAIGHT TALKING

January 2009, Jamaica

WHEN we arrived in the West Indies, I was feeling very motivated. I hadn't realised until I got the job how much I'd been waiting to do it, and I had a lot of ideas on how we could do things differently. The time felt right for me – others had been tried and this was my opportunity to put my stamp on things. I felt quite strongly that right from the start, I needed to tell the players how I wanted to operate, what I was about as a captain. I was full of energy and looking forward to it – though there was a bit of trepidation because the usual team structure had been disturbed. Andy Flower was playing a supporting role in his temporary position, and he was just looking to help out with the nets and organise things. In fact, he ended up doing a lot more over the course of the tour, but that was certainly the case at the start. So there was a great deal on my shoulders, but I was excited about it.

Before we came up with the charter I'd sat down and thought long and hard about where I felt we'd gone wrong over the last couple of years, and where we needed to change things. Central to it all was responsibility. It had become a bit of a crutch for players to say, 'Ah, well, Mooresy told me to do this, or Flower told me to do that, or Ottis Gibson told me to do that, and it hasn't worked.' I wanted to get away from that completely and move to a situation where the coaches were almost like consultants that the players could go to for advice about things they were struggling with – not the other way around, with the coaches telling the players what to do all the time. It's very simple, really. There's no one out there in the middle with you, and you need to be able to adapt your game and make decisions under pressure; you've got to get used to making decisions about your game on a daily basis – nothing more complicated than that. I also had some thoughts about the style of cricket we wanted to play.

The players responded really well. They wanted to believe in something and move beyond where we'd been, and they loved the idea of being given responsibility. At that stage, I was talking about having a lot of optional bits to practise. It doesn't have to be formulaic all the time – find what it is you need rather than want to do, and do it. We also gave players more responsibility off the pitch in terms of looking after themselves and the amount of alcohol they drank and so on. There were a lot of teething problems, but the players really warmed to the general attitude. The results didn't come in that first tour, though.

I've spoken quite a lot to the sports psychologist Steve Bull over the years, and he's always been helpful on leadership. He bangs on about how you can never have too much communication – so communicate. He does a lot of work in the corporate sector, and he says the biggest mistake people make is they think that because they've told someone something once, it's gone in – whereas you have to continue communicating all the time. That's a bit difficult for me, because I'm not a constant talker, I'm more of a thinker. It's something I have to work on, but fortunately between myself and Andy I think we cover it reasonably well.

Players want to feel that they belong to something and that their role in it is recognised – that what they're going through is appreciated. So if they're having a tough time, I think it gives them a huge lift if you say, 'Mate, I know it's tough – I've been there, it's not fun. Obviously we've got to find a way of getting out of it.' Because often in that situation, people ignore you or tiptoe around you because they don't know what to say. That's certainly one of Andy's real strengths – he has those difficult conversations with people, and people respond to it.

I'd learnt a lot from Michael Vaughan. He was an exceptional captain – the way he dealt with people, his unflappable nature. He was a very good communicator and filled people with confidence, but I wasn't him. I had different strengths. He seemed to do things on feel a lot, whereas I think things through more. While I was in the West Indies, I also took the opportunity to go out for dinner with Mike Atherton and Nasser Hussain and a few others, and chatted through the various challenges facing the England cricket team, such as the media, the counties, the ECB – all the stuff that I was still a little naive about at that stage.

There are a few books about leadership that have struck a chord with me over the years. Mike Brearley's *The Art of Captaincy* is definitely one. I read it a long time ago and I've reread it since. Another is Clive Woodward's book about England's Rugby World Cup success, *Winning!* Then there's *The Coach* by Ric Charlesworth, who coached the Australian Hockeyroos and played cricket for Western Australia. He's also been the New Zealand high performance manager, and a politician. His book contains some really interesting ideas and I remember noting a lot of it down. He talks about never sitting on a lead, and how he didn't really have a captain in his teams – he believed in the players all taking responsibility. Some of the seeds of what I was thinking came from his book.

8 February, Royal Antigua Hotel

We were humiliated in Jamaica. It was the worst possible start – the West Indies at this stage were quite a moderate side, so to be rolled over in that fashion was very disappointing. We had a meeting the next day and got out a lot of the stuff that had been simmering away under the surface. Andy Flower was brilliant – it was the moment that we all realised that he had something special. He was very honest about his own views and some of the things that he hadn't said before, and then he encouraged other people to talk, but did it in a way that was very constructive and sympathetic to their point of view. So it wasn't 'You're saying something I don't agree with, so you're talking rubbish.' It was 'Okay, that's interesting – I don't necessarily agree with it, but I can see why you're saying that.' A lot came up about the players not having bought into the team side of things. There were some pretty hard conversations going on.

It was the first time for ages that we'd had any real honesty in our dressing room. A good example would be that before, when a player got out playing a dumb shot, everyone in the dressing room would say, 'What the hell is he doing? That's just so stupid.' But when he came in they'd just say, 'Unlucky, mate,' and that would be the end of it. Now we were saying, 'Look – we've got a problem with the way you keep getting out like that.' There was a lot that needed to come out.

When we left that room I thought, 'Wow, that's a breath of fresh air. We've got things off our chest. We can move forward now.' We all had to take some stuff on the chin, things that people didn't like about us or felt we could do differently. But in the space of one meeting we'd gone from a team that never said anything honest, to one in which people could say almost anything to each other. It was early days, but it was a massive hurdle to overcome and we got rid of a lot of the baggage that we'd been carrying with us for a number of years.

February–April

We drew the next three games, but we played all the cricket in them. I made quite a few runs, which helped to legitimise my position, showing that I could combine batting and captaincy. It added weight to what I said to the players and also showed that I could lead by example, which I think is an important part of leadership. In that series we had the West Indies nine down in Antigua and eight down in Trinidad, while the game in Barbados petered out, so we played some good cricket. Graeme Swann came into the side at the expense of Monty Panesar as it evolved during the course of the tour, and we ended up winning the one-day series that followed.

It was important for everyone that we got something out of that tour – for myself and Andy Flower to be able to say, 'Look, we've achieved something here. It's only a small achievement, a one-day series, but it's something to work with, and we've got a huge summer coming up.' For me the great thing was that I found I loved doing the job – every minute of it. I loved the decision-making, I loved the stresses and strains, I loved having to think about other things except just batting, and it filled me with a lot of confidence and excitement for what was to come that summer against the Aussies.

When we got back to England, the ECB held an interview process for the coaching job. I was asked for my thoughts, but I wasn't directly involved in the process, and rightly so, because I would have to work with whoever was brought in. But I'd got on outstandingly with Andy on that tour. Andy also wants to lead by example – by how he holds himself and talks to people. By then he had become clear in his own mind that it was a job he wanted to do and felt capable of doing, whereas at the start he had had worries about usurping Peter Moores. Over the course of the tour he had developed a strong appetite for the job.

It was a relief when it was announced that he'd got the position, because we'd started something together. It would have been tough to go back to square one with someone else. But I felt it was absolutely right that the ECB should have that interview process – in contrast to Peter Moores, where the Board decided on an early appointment having recently concluded interviews with the leading candidates for a senior position at Loughborough. But this time Andy was indisputably the right man. The great thing about him was that we had enormous respect for what he'd achieved as a player himself. That's very important at the start of your tenure, because it means people will listen. If what you say is rubbish, they'll stop listening, of course – but it's far harder to earn respect having not had it in the first place.

June 2009, Ypres
We took the squad on a trip to Ypres in Belgium. It was Andy Flower's idea. He felt it was in keeping with what we were trying to do with the side, in terms of spreading our horizons and getting to know each other better as people rather than just as cricketers. He thought that it was important to put what we were doing into context and to appreciate what other people had been through representing their country, albeit in extreme circumstances. The Aussies had done something

similar before, and for the most part the players were brilliant. They really got something out of it.

It was very emotional – we went to the grave of a man who had played for England and Kent called Colin Blythe, who died at Passchendaele. The defining moment was the Menin Gate. They have a service every day. We sat there quietly and I laid a wreath. The thing that struck me most was that it was almost 100 years after it had all taken place, and there were still 500 people there every day. You realised that if those men in their graves could see what was happening, they'd be very proud of what they'd done for their country, and very proud that people still remembered them doing it.

I was watching to see how the other players reacted, because I was worried that people might be very cynical. Certainly in the past other England sides would have been, but I didn't see much evidence of it. The main thing was that the guys enjoyed it. It brought us closer together as a group and it steeled us for what was to come in the Ashes series. There were bound to be a lot of things that would try to push us apart as a side over the coming weeks, and warfare drives home the importance of sticking together. It was going to be harder for the Aussies to break us down.

England in the West Indies 2008–09

Tests – The Wisden Trophy
1st Test. Sabina Park, Kingston, Jamaica. 4–7 February 2009
England 318 (K.P. Pietersen 97, M.J. Prior 64, S.J. Benn 4–77) and 51 (J.E. Taylor 5–11, S.J. Benn 4–31)
West Indies 392 (R.R. Sarwan 107, C.H. Gayle 104, S.C.J. Broad 5–85)
West Indies won by an innings and 23 runs.

2nd Test. Sir Vivian Richards Stadium, North Sound, Antigua. 13 February 2009
England 7–0
Match abandoned after 10 balls because of dangerous outfield.

3rd Test. Antigua Recreation Ground, St John's, Antigua. 15–19 February 2009
England 566–9 dec (A.J. Strauss 169, P.D. Collingwood 113) and 221–8 dec (A.N. Cook 58)
West Indies 285 (R.R. Sarwan 94, G.P. Swann 5–57) and 370–9 (R.R. Sarwan 106, S.C.J. Broad 3–69)
Match drawn.

4th Test. Kensington Oval, Bridgetown, Barbados. 26 February–2 March 2009
England 600–6 dec (A.J. Strauss 142, R.S. Bopara 104, P.D. Collingwood 96) and 279–2 dec (A.N. Cook 139*)
West Indies 749–9 dec (R.R. Sarwan 291, D. Ramdin 166, G.P. Swann 5–165)
Match drawn.

5th Test. Queen's Park Oval, Port of Spain, Trinidad. 6–10 March 2009
England 546–6 dec (P.D. Collingwood 161, A.J. Strauss 142, M.J. Prior 131*) and 237–6 dec (K.P. Pietersen 102)
West Indies 544 (S. Chanderpaul 147*, B.P. Nash 109, C.H. Gayle 102) and 114–8 (G.P. Swann 3–13, J.M. Anderson 3–24)
Match drawn.

West Indies won the series 1–0.

One-Day Internationals
1st ODI. Providence Stadium, Guyana. 20 March 2009
England 270–7 (50 overs); West Indies 244–7 (46.2 overs)
England won by 1 run (D/L method).

2nd ODI. Providence Stadium, Guyana. 22 March 2009
West Indies 264–8 (50 overs); England 243 (48.2 overs)
West Indies won by 21 runs.

3rd ODI. Kensington Oval, Bridgetown, Barbados. 27 March 2009
England 117 (41.3 overs); West Indies 117–2 (14.4 overs)
West Indies won by 8 wickets (D/L method).

4th ODI. Kensington Oval, Bridgetown, Barbados. 29 March 2009
West Indies 239–9 (50 overs); England 136–1 (18.3 overs)
England won by 9 wickets (D/L method).

5th ODI. Beausejour Stadium, Gros Islet, St Lucia. 3 April 2009
England 172–5 (29 overs); West Indies 146 (28 overs)
England won by 26 runs.

England won the series 3–2.

4

WINNING AT HOME

12 July 2009, Cardiff, 1st Test, day 5

Wow, what a day! We managed to grab a draw out of the jaws of defeat, and it was down to players we'd never relied on with the bat before, the likes of Anderson, Panesar and Swann. For me it marked the turning of a corner. From then on, winning the home Ashes series seemed possible.

Andy Flower and I sat there watching it unfold. Halfway through the final day we were talking about how we could bounce back at Lord's if we lost the game. Then suddenly we were counting down the overs, then counting down the balls, and it was amazing. At first, there was just a flicker of belief that we could pull off a draw, but we needed something extraordinary to happen. That belief grew and grew, until it was knocked down a peg when we lost Swann and Collingwood, leaving Anderson and Panesar to see out eleven overs, which nobody expected them to do.

Then as the overs passed, we began to think, 'Hang on, they're looking quite comfortable here.' Hauritz was bowling and turning the ball away from their bats, so unless they nicked one, it was going to be quite hard for them to get out. I was trying to convey an air of confidence and belief, but deep down I was finding it very tough to watch, very tough. Ultimately, we just managed to hang on. It showed how much we had come together as a team. It really gave us impetus to move forward and make further strides.

We'd been in Australia's position against India a couple of years before at Lord's: we'd had them nine down, then an lbw decision which we all thought was out wasn't given, and they escaped. A few days later they beat us comprehensively at Trent Bridge. If you've played all the cricket in the game and come away with nothing, you feel robbed and that you haven't got what you deserved. But if you have just escaped despite playing no cricket, you think, 'Hey, look what's happened, we've got away with it, it's back to square one, we haven't lost anything.' That is a much better position mentally going into the next game.

16–20 July, Lord's, 2nd Test

So it proved at Lord's. We won a very important toss, the wicket was flat and it was a lovely sunny day. They were deflated, and tired after spending a lot of time on the field at Cardiff. Mitchell Johnson didn't bowl very well, and we got off to a bit of a flyer. Then suddenly we started believing again: 'Hold on, we're in a great position in this game – we can go on and win it.' And through Freddie Flintoff, we did.

By the time the 2009 Ashes came along, Fred felt something of an outsider. He'd spent a great deal of time away injured during the previous two years. A lot of his close mates had been discarded or moved on or retired, so he didn't feel like the fulcrum of the side any more – he felt as if he was popping in now and again. When you throw into the mix that he had announced he was going to retire at the end of the series, it was almost a farewell tour. What tends to happen with players in that situation is that they concentrate on doing as well as they can for their last few Test matches, but they're probably not as in tune with what the side is trying to do long-term, and they're probably not as interested in it either, because they've only a few games to go. So his time as the main performer in the team and the guy around which other guys played was more in 2003 and 2004–05 than in 2009.

We had performed well without him a lot over the previous two years, so none of us felt we couldn't. There was a whole media circus that surrounded him – 'What will England do without Freddie?' 'Is Freddie fit for this game?' It was quite annoying, but it wasn't his fault. It was just the way the media reacted to him. They like to build up one or two players – 'These are the great players and these are the players that create the stories.' What we were trying to do was not to have one or two great players – we wanted to have eleven players who all performed. So I think Freddie retiring gave us a pretty blank canvas from which to work. But it was still a great bowling performance at Lord's to see us home. Fast and furious. One of the most sustained pieces of fast bowling I have seen.

20–23 August, The Oval, 5th Test

Australia were favourites to take the final Test after hammering us at Headingley. Once again, winning the toss at The Oval was crucial. Right from ball one there were signs that this might be our time. It was incredible, thinking back to where we'd been nine months or so previously. To win the Ashes series against a good Australian side was an amazing achievement. We probably didn't have the belief to begin with, so we surprised ourselves a little. The 2009 series won't be remembered as fondly as 2005, and rightly so, because the Australian side weren't as great and there hadn't been such a long gap without winning the Ashes, but for those of us who were in it, it was incredibly satisfying. There were a lot of young guys who hadn't played in 2005, and a few who had just played in 2006–07 when we were beaten, and now we had proved to ourselves that we could be a good cricket team. We'd lost a lot of that belief in the eighteen months before that. Then there was my own personal achievement of winning an Ashes series as captain – not many have managed to do that. It convinced me that we were on the right track and that if we'd done it once, there was no reason why we couldn't do it again.

We celebrated in a private room in our hotel, and all the families were there. Compared to the 2005 victory celebrations, where everyone got off their faces and disappeared to different parts of London, I thought it was much better that we were all together as a group, for a certain amount of time at least, and that we involved the families, because the families had been through so much with us. So for me personally it was a better celebration than 2005 – though I'm sure other people may disagree.

Australia in England 2009

Tests – The Ashes

1st Test. SWALEC Stadium, Cardiff. 8–12 July 2009
England 435 (K.P. Pietersen 69, M.G. Johnson 3–87) and 252–9 (P.D. Collingwood 74, B.W. Hilfenhaus 3–47)
Australia 674–6 dec (R.T. Ponting 150, M.J. North 125, S.M. Katich 122, B.J. Haddin 121)
Match drawn.

2nd Test. Lord's, London. 16–20 July 2009
England 425 (A.J. Strauss 161, A.N. Cook 95, B.W. Hilfenhaus 4–103) and 311–6 dec (M.J. Prior 61)
Australia 215 (M.E.K. Hussey 51, J.M. Anderson 4–55) and 406 (M.J. Clarke 136, B.J. Haddin 80, A. Flintoff 5–92)
England won by 115 runs.

3rd Test. Edgbaston, Birmingham. 30 July–3 August 2009
Australia 263 (S.R. Watson 62, J.M. Anderson 5–80, G. Onions 4–58) and 375–5 (M.J. Clarke 103*, M.J. North 96)
England 376 (A. Flintoff 74, A.J. Strauss 69, B.W. Hilfenhaus 4–109)
Match drawn.

4th Test. Headingley, Leeds. 7–9 August 2009
England 102 (P.M. Siddle 5–21) and 263 (G.P. Swann 62, S.C.J. Broad 61, M.G. Johnson 5–69)
Australia 445 (M.J. North 110, M.J. Clarke 93, S.C.J. Broad 6–91)
Australia won by an innings and 80 runs.

5th Test. The Oval, London. 20–23 August 2009
England 332 (I.R. Bell 72, A.J. Strauss 55, P.M. Siddle 4–75) and 373–9 dec (I.J.L. Trott 119, A.J. Strauss 75, M.J. North 4–98)
Australia 160 (S.M. Katich 50, S.C.J. Broad 5–37, G.P. Swann 4–38) and 348 (M.E.K. Hussey 121, G.P. Swann 4–120)
England won by 197 runs.

England won the series 2–1.

5

HURDLES

November–December 2009, South Africa

At the end of that summer in England we had been beaten 6–1 in the one-day series by Australia, and Andy Flower and I sat down and said, 'We've got to do things differently in one-day cricket. What we've been doing hasn't worked, it hasn't worked for years, so we've got to change it around.' So for the one-day series in South Africa before the Test series we brought in some different players, and we came up with the strategy of playing very aggressively with the bat, but also trying to take wickets by being deadly accurate. We did not have a mystery bowler or a guy who could bowl at 95 miles an hour to take wickets in the middle of an innings, so we needed bowlers who were accurate and skilful with their changes of pace, and they needed to be backed up by a first-rate fielding performance, with potential ones stopped, boundaries turned into twos, run-outs pulled off. There's no point in the bowlers building up pressure if that pressure is released by the fielding unit.

The strategy worked in the warm-up games. It worked at Centurion, where we limited South Africa to a very manageable score, and it worked at Port Elizabeth, where we bowled them out very cheaply. It was part of our evolution as a cricket side, and it also confirmed that our bowlers were a match for anyone in the world in terms of consistency and accuracy – and importantly they'd demonstrated it away from home with a Kookaburra ball. Stuart Broad, Jimmy Anderson and Tim Bresnan were all excellent. And Graeme Swann did his usual good job. It was noticeable that South Africa struggled to get them away.

Anderson's consistency made you think, 'Wow, this bloke has really improved.' The perception of Jimmy Anderson was that he was as good as anyone in the world when the conditions were in his favour and the ball was swinging, but get him away from home and he was expensive and struggled to make any breakthroughs. He could appear to be the weak link in the attack in those circumstances. Sometimes his body language was poor too. In South Africa he proved to everyone that he was now a very different proposition.

First, he was far more accurate, with great control over various deliveries. But he also had a Plan B – he didn't just bowl big away-swingers and hope it would swing. He could bowl in-swingers, he could bowl cutters, he could mix up his pace; suddenly he was a bowler that batsmen couldn't just set themselves against. They were always wondering what was coming next. He's still got a quick bouncer, but in some ways he's learnt to bowl within himself. He's no longer that young tearaway fast-bowler, but the leader of the pack, the smart guy, dispensing advice to the other bowlers – in much the same way as Matthew Hoggard did at the end of his England career.

It was a gradual process, but I noticed a definite difference when Flintoff wasn't there. Jimmy had had to step up numerous times when Flintoff was injured, and certainly once he retired, Jimmy became the leader of the attack. So his mindset was very different. He loves standing at mid-on and talking to Broady or Tim Bresnan about the game situation and what they are trying to do to the batsmen. It became clear to us all that here was someone with a great cricket brain. He didn't just bowl his ten overs in a one-dayer and then disappear to the boundary – he actually wanted to be involved in everything, in strategy, in the fielding, and he loved being a senior player. By the end of the South Africa tour he had become very much the lynchpin of our bowling attack.

7 January 2010, Cape Town, 3rd Test, day 5

I was sitting on the balcony, having just seen Graham Onions face the final delivery from Morne Morkel. We were nine wickets down, and for the second time in the series he'd got us through to the end. I looked around at the other players and they were all jumping up and down with joy. One of the things we had talked about at Cardiff and Centurion was that we shouldn't celebrate a draw, because obviously we haven't won, and in both those circumstances that was right, but here we'd reached an unbeatable position in the four-match series, and it felt right to celebrate it. We'd dug as deep as any side possibly could for two out of the last three games and managed to hang on against some really world-class bowling from Dale Steyn and Morkel. The guys had shown their character again. As a team, we were greater than the sum of our parts. Rather than hoping that someone would perform when it really mattered, players were stepping up to the plate as a matter of course and delivering when all logic dictated that they wouldn't.

Going into that final day in Cape Town, we were three wickets down, so they had the whole day to bowl us out. We had no chance of victory, and usually in those circumstances it is just a matter of time before a side collapses. The wicket was pacy and uneven, so South Africa held all the aces in the pack; we had nothing but hope to keep us going. Collingwood played an unbelievable innings – the sort we had come to expect from him. Ian Bell showed his development with a really important innings under pressure. He definitely wanted to prove to his team-mates more than anything that he was capable of producing an innings like that, rather than just scoring runs when the going was easy.

Escape from that situation in a Test match once, and there's a lot of relief at dodging a bullet. Do it two or three times, and you begin to see it as a strength – we've done it before, and we're likely to do it again. The more you see the team unit working successfully, the more faith people have in it, and the more they're willing to give to the team as a result. We really saw that in the way Ian Bell matured as a cricketer. He was under pressure going into that series – huge pressure – and he turned it around. Alastair Cook made some runs after a bad trot, and Paul Collingwood played some very valuable innings.

Suddenly we weren't relying on the likes of KP as much as we used to. He had a bit of a tough series – I didn't have a great one myself – but it didn't matter because we were getting performances from other members of the side. Anderson had a good tour, Graham Onions was outstanding, although he didn't get the wickets he deserved, and Swann proved what an effective performer he could be away from home. So the draw in Cape Town was a massive moment for us. We weren't able to go on and win the series in Johannesburg, but South Africa, who were the number one side in the world – at the start of the series anyway – had failed to beat us on their home turf. It was an achievement every bit as impressive as winning the Ashes in 2009.

England in South Africa 2009–10

One-Day Internationals
1st ODI. New Wanderers Stadium, Johannesburg. 20 November 2009
Match abandoned without a ball being bowled.

2nd ODI. Centurion Park, Centurion. 22 November 2009
South Africa 250–9 (50 overs); England 252–3 (46 overs)
England won by 7 wickets.

3rd ODI. Newlands, Cape Town. 27 November 2009
South Africa 354–6 (50 overs); England 242 (41.3 overs)
South Africa won by 112 runs.

4th ODI. St George's Park, Port Elizabeth. 29 November 2009
South Africa 119 (36.5 overs); England 121–3 (31.2 overs)
England won by 7 wickets.

5th ODI. Kingsmead, Durban. 4 December 2009
Match abandoned without a ball being bowled.

England won the series 2–1.

Tests – The Basil D'Oliveira Trophy
1st Test. Centurion Park, Centurion. 16–20 December 2009
South Africa 418 (J.H. Kallis 120, G.P. Swann 5–110) and 301–7 dec (H.M. Amla 100, J.M. Anderson 4–73)
England 356 (G.P. Swann 85, P.L. Harris 5–123) and 228–9 (K.P. Pietersen 81, I.J.L Trott 69, F. de Wet 4–55)
Match drawn.

2nd Test. Kingsmead, Durban. 26–30 December 2009
South Africa 343 (G.C. Smith 75, J.H. Kallis 75, G.P. Swann 4–110) and 133 (G.P. Swann 5–54, S.C.J. Broad 4–43)
England 574–9 dec (I.R. Bell 140, A.N. Cook 118, P.D. Collingwood 91, M. Morkel 3–78)
England won by an innings and 98 runs.

3rd Test. Newlands, Cape Town. 3–7 January 2010
South Africa 291 (J.H. Kallis 108, J.M. Anderson 5–63) and 447–7 dec (G.C. Smith 183, H.M. Amla 95)
England 273 (M.J. Prior 76, A.N. Cook 65, M. Morkel 5–75) and 296–9 (I.R. Bell 78, A.N. Cook 55, P.L. Harris 3–85)
Match drawn.

4th Test. New Wanderers Stadium, Johannesburg. 14–17 January 2010
England 180 (P.D. Collingwood 47, D.W. Steyn 5–51) and 169 (P.D. Collingwood 71, M. Morkel 4–59)
South Africa 423–7 dec (G.C. Smith 105, M.V. Boucher 95, H.M. Amla 75, S.C.J. Broad 3–83)
South Africa won by an innings and 74 runs.

Series drawn 1–1.

6

RECHARGING THE BATTERIES

March 2010, Buninyong, Australia

WHILE the England squad went to Bangladesh I spent about four weeks at our house in Victoria. I felt that as I was having that time off, it was important to get my body in as good a shape as possible. So I spent an hour or two every day in the local gym in Ballarat. Occasionally a gym instructor would look at me suspiciously, as if thinking to himself, 'What the hell's the England captain doing in a gym in Ballarat?' And that was a fair question. Other than that it was a month of normality, playing with the kids, the kind of family life I hadn't had the opportunity to enjoy for a while. Our place is out in the country, quite a spacious plot with a tennis court and things for the kids to do, and there are lots of great runs in the bush and the woods.

It was the perfect place to get away from things and make sure I was ready for the challenge ahead. There was no one badgering me all the time and very few people recognised me. By the end of the South Africa tour I had become weary. After a very high-intensity Ashes series, we'd gone straight into the Champions Trophy in South Africa, then back again to South Africa for a tough five-one-day and four-Test tour. So there had been no break until then. And while I felt a long way from the team, it was also a bit of a godsend for me and my family that I had that opportunity.

Watching England play without me on TV felt strange. I didn't like it particularly. I was keeping in reasonably regular contact with Andy Flower, but it's still difficult not to feel like an outsider. You see the guys toiling away in Bangladesh and playing very well and having to dig deep, and part of you feels that you should be there with them.

I rang Andy one evening to see how things were going in Bangladesh, and I said to him, 'I'm just looking at the schedule for Middlesex for when I get back, and I think I should probably play all the games leading up to the first Test.' He replied, 'I think that's a good idea. Do you know there's been quite a lot of criticism in the media of your decision not to go to Bangladesh? It's important that you get playing again before the summer comes along.' Up to that point I hadn't read a thing. I knew that it wasn't likely to go down particularly well, so I'd purposely not looked at the papers. But hearing those words irritated me, even though I wasn't surprised by them.

The decision for me to miss Bangladesh was one that Andy and I had mulled over in South Africa. We'd looked at the England schedule for the next eighteen months. After the tour to Bangladesh a very busy and demanding English summer lay ahead – although we had only six Tests, against

Bangladesh again and Pakistan, the ECB had fitted in five one-day internationals against Australia. Then it was straight to Australia for the Ashes, followed by seven one-dayers and finally the World Cup in March 2011. The schedule was incredibly tough. We realised that if we wanted to peak for the Ashes and still be in a half-decent state by the time the World Cup came, we had to make sure that our key performers – the ones who played in all forms of the game – had some opportunity over that period for a rest, otherwise the bowlers were likely to get injuries, and at least one or two of the batsmen were likely to become mentally shot and perform inconsistently or lose form altogether.

I'm usually a good sleeper but there had been times in South Africa when I couldn't sleep at all. The cricket becomes all-encompassing after a while and there are so many little decisions you have to make. It does wear you out. I think the important thing was that I knew what was to come, and that it was going to be even tougher than what we'd just been through. I've seen and heard how past England captains became ground down by the job. Mike Atherton said it in his book and Nasser Hussain mentioned it in his as well. Michael Vaughan was in a very similar state of mind by the end of his tenure. I'd only been in the job for a year or so, but I recognised that if I wanted to do it well in Australia and at the World Cup, it was important to prioritise. So it was decided that I would miss the Bangladesh tour, along with Jimmy Anderson.

The attitude behind the criticism seemed to be that the captain should never leave his troops behind – he shouldn't ask them to do something that he isn't willing to do himself. I can understand that criticism. On the surface it seems very justified, but the counter-argument is that, with so much cricket, you have to prioritise what your goals are as a side. What series can you get away with not playing a full-strength side in? And if you accept that, it suddenly becomes a lot clearer that you can't expect people to play every game of cricket in a two-year period, because the likelihood is that they will become incredibly jaded. As a captain, the demands on your play are even greater, of course.

So I missed that Bangladesh tour because I believed very strongly that it was actually in the best interests of the England cricket team. Andy Flower agreed and the rest of the players understood. It wasn't about me not fancying a trip to Bangladesh. It was nothing like that. It was about our long-term strategy for winning the Ashes, and playing well at the World Cup. If we needed to take some criticism in order to achieve those goals then we were willing to do that.

The other benefit was that it gave Alastair Cook an opportunity to captain the side. It was very important for his development. But it was also crucial that we had someone who was able to take over if I got injured at any stage. He had obviously been marked as a potential successor to me. People respect him and he has a good cricket brain, but we didn't know a lot about him – how he would handle the pressures in the middle, how he would cope with the media, that sort of thing. So to make sure that we had every angle covered, it was essential to give Alastair that opportunity.

April–May

I played a lot for Middlesex at the start of the summer and had a bit of a shocker. I found it very difficult to readjust. It was the most intense county schedule of all time. They'd recently elongated the Twenty20 competition and were trying to finish the season early for the Champions League that followed, which meant that Middlesex were playing seven four-day games in seven weeks with quite a lot of one-day cricket thrown in as well. It was incredibly tough on the players to keep turning out performances anywhere near their best. I'm sure it was similar in the 1970s and 1980s, when two three-day games a week was the norm.

I came away from those seven weeks a little disappointed with my own form, though there were some extenuating circumstances. They'd done away with the heavy roller over the winter and that made the batting quite tricky, with the ball nipping all over the place. Also, I think it takes a while to adjust to county cricket again – in international cricket you get used to bowlers bowling at 90 miles an hour and suddenly you're facing guys bowling at 80 miles an hour, but very accurately and swinging it. Our wickets probably aren't as good as Test match wickets, either. You've got to adapt your game, and it took me a while to do that. At least I got some runs in my final game, against Surrey.

There are a lot of very good cricketers in county cricket and a lot of good sides, but playing that quantity of games does not allow players to prepare well enough. It doesn't allow bowlers to bowl at 100 per cent of their capability; it encourages batsmen to have the mindset that there's always an innings tomorrow or next week, rather than being focused on each innings. If you take the view that it should be a breeding ground for Test match cricketers, I can't help thinking that both the schedule and the quantity of cricket played in the county game need to be looked at. But, the financial pressures facing the Counties, who employ over 400 cricketers in England and Wales, are huge.

July, The Hyatt Hotel, Birmingham
This was the first of a series of dinners with groups of players to prepare for the tour of Australia. It was an idea suggested by the sports psychologist Steve Bull, and was something we had used effectively before the 2009 Ashes. We knew that the tour Down Under would ask even more questions of us as a side, not just on the pitch but off the field, dealing with the vagaries of touring life. So it was important that the players understood what we were likely to encounter, and that they also had the opportunity to have their say on how we should prepare for it.

The first dinner, during the Test series against Pakistan, was run by our new psychologist, Mark Bawden. The players were able to talk about anything that they thought might be relevant to winning the Ashes, whether it was how to bowl on Australian wickets, how to handle the Australian media or how to deal with sledging.

We talked about ways to make sure that the cricket didn't become too all-encompassing on the tour, to make sure that guys could relax and enjoy themselves, such as taking golf clubs on tour for the first time. We talked about not having newspapers in the dressing rooms or delivered to our rooms and hotels. We talked about the difficulties of being away from home for that length of time, away from family, and how we might deal with that together as a group rather than leaving people in isolation. We talked about our strengths as a side – it was really interesting to reaffirm those.

The idea of the dinners was specifically to put in everyone's mind what we were likely to encounter, so that we weren't surprised by anything when we got out there. The worst thing you can do when you're preparing for a big event is just to assume that things will go well. You have to assume that anything might happen, and work out how you might react, so that when the pressure is on and you have to act quickly, you've already thought about the potential solution. And that's an individual thing as well as a team thing.

Of course we wanted guys to throw ideas about as to how we might play out there, how we'd get the ball reversing, how we were going to deal with the cricket side of things. But we were also conscious that a successful tour is about so much more than that. It's about overcoming the various challenges that come your way away from home, whether it's the media getting on your case as a side, or having to deal with bad form.

We talked about the attitude we should take into the warm-up games – something that we hadn't done very successfully in the past – and the plans that we'd employ in the Test matches. Ultimately, it was the players who came up with them. That's so much more powerful than just being told what to do. It was an important part of the preparation and it was interesting to hear the range of opinions from the different people: from a guy who's played one Test, to one who's played eighty or ninety.

One of the discussion points was Twitter. We'd had some incidents over the summer when players had been caught out saying things on Twitter that they shouldn't have, and we had a choice to go one of two ways. One was to ban Twitter completely and therefore make sure that we didn't leak any information. The other was to say to those guys who use Twitter, 'Right, you realise that we can't have information coming out of our squad – what happens within the four walls of the dressing room is sacrosanct – so you draw up a code of conduct to make sure it doesn't happen,' and that's exactly what they did.

Personally, I don't understand the appeal – I don't think my life is interesting enough to broadcast to other people, and even if it was, I don't particularly like the idea of conversing with a load of people I don't know. It's just not my thing.

But I understand that other people view it very differently, and certainly the younger generation love checking Twitter at every opportunity, and that includes when you're sitting opposite them at a dinner. But maybe that says more about my company than their interest in Twitter.

7

STEPPING OVER
THE LINE

28 August 2010, Marlow

WE'D had a decent though tricky summer, with the ball darting about off some helpful pitches. We were coming towards the end of the Pakistan Test series and I was sitting on my sofa at home just flicking through the channels when I happened to watch the news headlines on the ten o'clock news. The lead story was that the *News of the World* had a scoop about the Lord's Test I was actually playing in being fixed. I was absolutely flabbergasted. Usually with this sort of story you have at least some idea before it's published, but I hadn't heard a thing.

I was shocked. I wasn't sure how things were likely to play out, or how much truth there was in the allegations, but I knew that the next day was going to be a particularly uncomfortable one. My gut reaction was that if the allegations were true, I didn't want to be on the same pitch as those guys. I felt violated, because we'd been putting so much time and effort into what was actually quite a tough Test series, even though we were 2–1 up at that stage. Now it appeared that some members of the other team weren't all that interested in winning the match – they were more concerned about making money out of it. So I was angry and frustrated, and more than a little curious about what was going to happen.

It had been a strange day. Broad and Trott made that massive world-record stand, rescuing us from 102 for seven, and then the Pakistanis were four or five down for nothing. I don't know if they had an inkling that it might have been coming out – I really don't know. I waited until midnight, when the actual *News of the World* piece came out, and read it thoroughly. The evidence seemed pretty damning.

When we arrived at Lord's on Sunday morning, the gist of the conversation was, 'Oh well, the cricket isn't important any more, and what Broad and Trott have done has been completely devalued.' We talked about what we should do, whether we should play or not. But ultimately we were in the middle of a Test match, and the only professional thing to do was to get on with the game and finish it off. The atmosphere between the two sides was icy-cold, but we simply had to go about our business.

It was one of the most underwhelming days of cricket I've ever played. When we took the wickets, we weren't even really celebrating them. We won the series – so what? We had to receive a trophy in the Long Room, which was a bit of a damp squib, and I had to field a thousand questions from journalists about the whole saga. It was going to take a while for us to regain our enthusiasm for playing against that side, and also for the stench of spot-fixing or match-fixing or whatever you want to call it to go away and allow players to concentrate on playing the game.

I hadn't had much of a relationship with Salman Butt. Up to that point he seemed to have done a fairly good job on the field with the players, though he was struggling with the bat, and we felt that he was a bit of a weak link in that respect. They'd been a competitive side and they were certainly up for the challenge – or so we thought. For a youngster like Amir potentially to be involved in it, for the captain potentially to be involved in it – it beggared belief.

My strong feeling was that the game of cricket had been dealt a pretty serious blow, and that everything we'd achieved in that series, and even in other series, had been devalued. It made us wonder whether it was an isolated incident, or whether it was more widespread. All the hours we'd spent in the gym and planning seemed pointless. And then what about our good individual performances? You can't help thinking, 'Well, was the guy at the other end not really trying to get me out, or did he have an ulterior motive?' And that's the problem – it makes you lose trust in the essence of cricket, which is a contest between two sides equally intent on winning the game.

It was clearly a great bit of journalism to bring it out in the open, but it was also an excellent opportunity for the ICC to dig deep and stamp out match-fixing once and for all. So in that sense I was certainly hopeful that some good might come out of it eventually, but it was going to put quite a few people's noses out of joint and take some tough decisions to achieve that.

September, one-day series v Pakistan

Nobody was enjoying having to play against Pakistan in those circumstances. Everything was still very raw and in a lot of ways unresolved from the Test matches. But we understood the situation, given that the three who were directly implicated in the Lord's Test had been stood down by the Pakistan team; we realised that the one-day series had to go ahead. But from the first ball, we would be fulfilling our obligations without feeling a great deal of excitement.

The first four games were joyless affairs. We won the first reasonably comfortably at Durham, put on a great chase at Headingley to go 2–0 up, then lost at The Oval. But even before the Oval game, there was talk of it not going ahead because of the ICC saying there were irregular betting patterns on a certain phase of the game. In fact, the newspapers came up with stuff like that throughout the one-day series – opening old cans of worms in Pakistan cricket, or referring to potential new allegations, about the Australia v Pakistan Test match, or from former Pakistani players.

So the cricket was completely overshadowed, and there was a very frosty relationship between the teams. At one stage in the Durham game Jonathan Trott said something to Kamran Akmal – nothing to do with match-fixing, something about running on the wicket – and Akmal reacted very volubly. It just showed the kind of stress he was under, and I had to step in to try to calm things down. I was saying to Kamran Akmal, 'He's within his rights to say something to you, mate – you can't react like that.' But the tensions were so high, and they were going to get higher.

The day before the fourth one-dayer – at Lord's – I was at home again when Ijaz Butt, the chairman of Pakistan Cricket Board, came out with the allegation that the England team might have been involved in some sort of illegal activity. I was absolutely furious when I saw what he'd said. It's one thing sticking up for your own players, it's quite another to accuse opposition teams of doing something untoward – even if it was careless language. It was particularly hard to take, given what we'd been through and that we'd agreed to continue the series. The chairman had obligations to the game of cricket, but he was clearly trying to deflect attention away from the Pakistan team. In doing so, he was calling our integrity into question, which was a very bitter pill to swallow, and I was particularly keen to make sure he wasn't allowed to get away with those comments. With the game less than twenty-four hours away, things had to move quickly. I spoke to Andy Flower about the situation.

Shortly afterwards, a meeting was called between myself, Andy Flower, Giles Clarke, David Collier and Hugh Morris to discuss the options available to us. We discussed the ramifications if we didn't play, the ramifications if we did play and what else we might do to make a stand, and there were differing viewpoints all around the table. The long and the short of it was that by the end Andy Flower and I had to have a series of meetings with the players to gauge how strong their opinions were as to whether we should play or not.

In the first meeting, many including myself felt that the best course of action was not to play the game; they'd called our integrity into question and that was a matter of principles, and you shouldn't forgo your principles for the sake of the money that the ECB might lose. Later we had a second meeting in which Giles Clarke, the ECB chairman, gave the reasons why he felt we should play the game. After that most of the players changed their opinion. It wasn't necessarily because of his arguments. I think we started to realise that our pulling out of the game would actually divert attention from Ijaz Butt and what the Pakistan team, or members of the Pakistan team, were alleged to have done, and turn it back onto ourselves and whether we'd done the right thing.

We appreciated that a full house, or close to a full house, was expected to turn up at Lord's the next day. It was also very late in the piece – at this stage it was almost eleven or twelve o'clock at night. Perhaps our obligations to the cricket-supporting public in our country and not wanting to be seen as the bad guys in this finally swayed the argument. In the end, we decided to play on the condition that we could issue our own statement, separately from the ECB. I then went away and wrote it, and met with Angus Porter from the PCA the next morning to tidy it up. We wanted to convey how deeply we felt about the comments, while at the same time continuing with the game as well as we could.

Unfortunately, things didn't die down immediately, because in the warm-up for the game Jonathan Trott and Wahab Riaz were involved in a scuffle. Certainly not many of our players had had much sleep the previous night, and I'm not sure what happened with the Pakistan players, but tensions were high. People were very emotional, and it only took a couple of words being exchanged before things blew up into a physical altercation. The first I knew about it was when Andy Flower came over to the dressing room and said, 'Have you heard what's happened with Trott?' Obviously Flower was very animated. He was disappointed that Trott had reacted in that manner, and he was disappointed that he had given the Pakistan team a chance to deflect attention away from themselves again. The match referee then said that the Pakistan side wouldn't play unless Trott apologised, and thankfully he was more than happy to do so. So the game got the go-ahead.

While this was going on, our players were warming up on their own without a captain or a coach. None of them was willing to play the game unless Trott played, and they were worried that he was going to be stood down, which is not something I would have wanted. But we finally got the game under way, and before going out I told the players, 'Listen, we can't afford to get emotional out here at all today. Even if we are five or ten per cent off our best, we've got to make sure we get through this game. Because if we let emotions run high, things could get very messy in the middle very quickly.'

It was a horrible game of cricket – I don't think any of the twenty-two players were particularly on their game. Perhaps Pakistan handled it slightly better than us, although we were in with a great chance of winning at one stage. But under lights our chase faltered and Pakistan ended up taking the game and levelling the series.

22 September, Rose Bowl, 5th ODI

With the series at 2–2, this was the decider. We turned up with the attitude that we just had to win the game, for all sorts of reasons. This time the guys were completely switched on. It wasn't an easy game of cricket – we relied heavily on Eoin Morgan to set us a defendable target – but as we went out on the field that final time I said to the players, 'Right, now the gloves are off. We don't have to keep our emotions in check any more – we've got to win this game at all costs.'

Everyone saw a far more passionate display from us. You could see when we celebrated our wickets how much it meant to us, and after we'd taken the final wicket, the satisfaction of winning the series was as good as anything I've experienced on a cricket field. We'd been brought a lot closer by another shared experience. It wasn't a good experience, but it prepared us well for what was to come in the winter. We knew we were going to be tested on and off the pitch in Australia, and we'd managed to come through a very tough three-week period with our dignity intact, playing the game in the right spirit and without falling out over what course of action to take. That evening the team song was sung with greater passion than I've ever known.

The Pakistan one-day series had the potential to destabilise our development as a team, but in the end it was probably quite a good test of it. It was something none of us had experienced before. Certainly as a captain I was tested as never before, and it seems to me that past England teams might have reacted differently towards it. There would have been far more disagreement in the ranks about what to do, with players entrenched in their views, sticking with their opinion no matter what. What happened this time was that there were plenty of different opinions, but we all came together knowing that it was for the greater good of the team. If it meant some players had to play when they felt uncomfortable about it, they were willing to do it. That was a great testament to how highly people valued the team above the individual.

Pakistan in England 2010

Tests

1st Test. Trent Bridge, Nottingham. 29 July–1 August 2010
England 354 (E.J.G. Morgan 130, M. Asif 5–77) and 262–9 dec (M.J. Prior 102*, U. Gul 3–41)
Pakistan 182 (U. Gul 65*, J.M. Anderson 5–54, S.T. Finn 3–50) and 80 (J.M. Anderson 6–17)
England won by 354 runs.

2nd Test. Edgbaston, Birmingham. 6–9 August 2010
Pakistan 72 (J.M. Anderson 4–20, S.C.J. Broad 4–38) and 296 (Z. Haider 88, G.P. Swann 6–65)
England 251 (K.P. Pietersen 80, I.J.L. Trott 55, S. Ajmal 5–82) and 118–1 (I.J.L. Trott 53*)
England won by 9 wickets.

3rd Test. The Oval, London. 18–21 August 2010
England 233 (M.J. Prior 84*, W. Riaz 5–63) and 222 (A.N. Cook 110, M. Amir 5–52)
Pakistan 308 (A. Ali 92*, M. Yousuf 56, G.P. Swann 4–68) and 148–6 (S. Butt 48, G.P Swann 3–50)
Pakistan won by 4 wickets.

4th Test. Lord's, London. 26–29 August 2010
England 446 (I.J.L Trott 184, S.C.J. Broad 169, M. Amir 6–84)
Pakistan 74 (G.P. Swann 4–12) and 147 (f/o) (U. Akmal 79*, G.P. Swann 5–62)
England won by an innings and 225 runs.

England won the series 3–1.

One-Day Internationals – NatWest Series

1st ODI. Riverside Ground, Chester-le-Street. 10 September 2010
England 274–6 (41 overs); Pakistan 250–9 (41 overs)
England won by 24 runs.

2nd ODI. Headingley, Leeds. 12 September 2010
Pakistan 294–8 (50 overs); England 295–6 (49.3 overs)
England won by 4 wickets.

3rd ODI. The Oval, London. 17 September 2010
Pakistan 241 (49.4 overs); England 218 (45.4 overs)
Pakistan won by 23 runs.

4th ODI. Lord's, London. 20 September 2010
Pakistan 265–7 (50 overs); England 227 (46.1 overs)
Pakistan won by 38 runs.

5th ODI. The Rose Bowl, Southampton. 22 September 2010
England 256–6 (50 overs); Pakistan 135 (37 overs)
England won by 121 runs.

England won the series 3–2.

8

AHEAD OF THE GAME

September 2010, Bavaria

STRAIGHT after that victory we found ourselves on a plane to Germany. I knew we were going to Munich, but none of the other players knew anything at all. There was a lot of speculation about our destination. We needed our passports, so people were assuming it was away from England. But we were told to bring very little gear – nothing to go out in, some swimming shorts, some hiking boots. It was an odd one for our families, knowing they couldn't contact us and not sure where we were going, but the good thing about it was that all the players had to concentrate on was getting through those five days. There was nothing else to think about, and in the middle of nowhere on a campsite with no electricity, it felt a world away from our lives as international cricketers.

The evening of the first day was the most memorable. We were sitting in a clearing in the forest, each and every one of us exhausted to the core, wet through and knowing that we'd gone as far as we thought we could go as individuals, but again we hadn't left anyone behind. We had arrived at Gatwick Airport between 1 a.m. and 3 a.m., after the PCA dinner, and had to be ready for a 4.30 meeting before taking the 6 a.m. flight to Munich. We were met there by members of the Australian police force and driven to an isolated woodland area in the middle of Bavaria. Then we got straight out of the minivan, put all our belongings in a backpack and just walked off into the woods.

We didn't know what was expected of us; we didn't know whether the idea was for us to learn new skills or just trek around, or whether we'd be doing physical work; we knew nothing. And from the moment we got there we realised that any idea that it might be a bit of fun was well wide of the mark. For the next seven or eight hours we were running up and down hills. This was with our management in tow as well – so we had to help them up the hills.

We were wearing just T-shirts and trousers and walking boots. It was pretty cold. I don't think it actually rained that day, but it did the next. The final insult was being handed two bricks each at about 3 p.m., and for the next three hours we had to run or walk with those bricks in our hands without allowing them to drop, while every kilometre or so having to stop and do exercises – either shoulder presses or press-ups with the bricks. It was the most painful thing I've ever done. They were bricks without anything to grip on to, so you had to clasp them to keep them in your hand. It was agony.

By the end of the day we were completely and utterly exhausted. We'd probably trekked 25 miles or so, done 1,000 press-ups, carried bricks for about 10 kilometres. We weren't allowed to speak to each other – it was pretty much hell on earth. We were all questioning whether it was such a great idea. It was originally Reg Dickason, the ECB security adviser, who came up with it. Australia had done it previously, and there was a feeling at the time – this was probably twelve months previously – that we needed to be more resilient as a side.

Things didn't improve much over the next few days, although by the end, having knocked us down to a very low place, they started building us up again, and we did some abseiling and had a few beers on the last night. But it was interesting – not just the physical work we did, but getting to know each other a lot better as people. We had sessions around bonfires talking about our lives away from cricket; it all makes you richer as a person and tighter as a group.

It was instructive to see how people coped. There were some quite unexpected results – guys who you didn't think would do that well surprised you, and vice versa. But we all got through it, which was the main thing. I remember thinking, 'This is hell on earth. We've survived one day – what's to come?' It was the sort of tiredness that you hear about but you don't often experience yourself, when you're absolutely shot of everything, and this was a group of generally pretty pampered cricketers, going to a place where none of us had been before.

October, Loughborough

About a week before we flew to Australia we all met up at Loughborough for our final pre-tour medical screening and fitness test. It's a day you dread because you're concerned that you're not as fit as you should be, and you're worried that this might just be a bad day for you, that you haven't eaten properly or you might get some strange asthma attack and humiliate yourself in front of your team-mates. The tests that players are always most worried about are the bleep test and the fat test. These days we have a set of twenty-five criteria that you have to reach a certain standard on, but if you're down in your bleep test or your fat test you're going to be subject to some unpleasant attention from the conditioning coach over the next couple of weeks. Happily, everyone got through it okay.

The one session that really stood out involved the batsmen splitting into two teams and playing a game against each other. There were a number of imaginary situations we had to deal with as a team, with Andy Flower firing balls from a bowling machine at a ridiculous pace and swinging them both ways. We had to find ways of either facing twenty balls, not getting out or making a certain number of runs. It was incredibly tough and definitely challenged your bravery.

The undisputed king of that game was Kevin Pietersen, who seemed to be able to play on a completely different plane to the rest of us. Kevin had had a lean spell leading up to the

Ashes tour, but we all looked at each other and thought, 'This guy is still an amazing cricketer to be able to do what he's doing against that bowling machine.' Most of us couldn't lay a bat on the ball. I think it did a lot for his confidence to realise that while others were struggling, he still had the ability to do something that was out of the ordinary.

The bowlers went through a number of drills, which was the first opportunity they'd had to bowl outside for a while. And we were also able to go out and have a couple of beers at the end of the first night. Having been in each other's company so much over the summer and during the camp in Germany, this wasn't really about spending a lot of time together – it was more about dotting the i's and crossing the t's in our final preparations before heading to Australian soil.

We also had some sessions with ProBatter, a bowling machine with a real bowler's run-up and delivery projected onto a screen at the front. It takes a bit of time to get used to. You still have a slight delay as the ball supposedly comes out of his hand, and it's a little bit hard to pick up the length of the ball to start with, but the more you use it, the more value you get out of it. For me, the great advantage is that you can time your trigger movements as the bowler – be it Johnson, Hilfenhaus or whoever – is coming in. It's something that's always very difficult against a standard bowling machine. And also the machine can bowl you different-length balls without you getting the cue from the operator pushing the machine up or down, so it can be more of a realistic test.

Clive Woodward said in his book that he wanted the England rugby team to have absolutely everything in place before the 2003 World Cup. They wanted to be the team by which all others were measured, in terms of facilities, coaching specialists and equipment. The England cricket team were getting close to that. No other team in the world had ProBatter, and it helped add to the feeling that maybe we were slightly ahead of the game for a change, rather than trying to catch up with the others, especially Australia, who always used to lead in that field in the past.

29 October, Departure

As usual there was a captain's press conference prior to leaving for Australia. I've never had to think too much about what I'm going to say – you generally go with the flow and try to be as honest as possible. But I got the feeling that that press conference was, if not the start of the phoney war, then one of the pivotal points of the phoney war. I knew that anything I said would be analysed and deciphered, and that people would look for signs of weakness or aggression or hints that we were going to do things differently.

It was the most pressurised press conference I've done, trying to get across that we weren't intimidated by going to Australia, that we were excited about it, but also that we wanted to play cricket in the right way, in the right spirit. One thing I said was that I didn't see why we'd be having a drink with the Australians during the series after each game. That was something to be done once the series had finished – until then you're two sets of players at war with each other. It was taken by the press as meaning we were going to war with Australia, and that was actually a slip of the tongue, which I regretted. But it made me realise what we had to deal with. This was different from any other series in terms of the attention people would give to every word, every practice session, every Twitter statement; the level of interest would be greater than ever before.

It was one of those situations where you feel under pressure to come out with exactly the right tone, and although you know that the press conference before you get on the plane should have no bearing whatsoever on the outcome of the Ashes, as a captain it's important that you try to set that tone and get the tour off to a good start.

9

SETTING THE TONE

30 October 2010, Arrival

THE thing that always strikes you when you arrive in Australia is the light – walking out of the airport and seeing the bright sunlight. In Perth it's always hot and you gain an understanding very quickly of the harshness of the conditions – it's a very dry, arid place. But for once that harshness wasn't matched by the people. They were very welcoming. Some of the lads went out for a few drinks that night and without exception they all reported comments like 'Good on ya, lads, you're playing great cricket, go and enjoy yourselves,' and they were all impressed by the friendliness of the people they'd met.

It was very different when we arrived in 2006. Everywhere we went, the country was united in wanting to gain revenge for losing in 2005. They still had their great team in place and the public were very confident that in their own conditions they were going to win. Right from the start of the tour we struggled. This time a lot of people in Australia didn't seem to believe their team were that good any more. They'd lost the Ashes in England, they'd just lost to India and they were struggling against Sri Lanka in a one-day series. A lot of people were saying, 'Yeah, I think you've got us this time. Good luck, enjoy your tour.' It was something I was unaccustomed to hearing from Australians. It was a bit of an eye-opener, definitely.

The defeat to India seemed to have reignited all the issues in their team. They were worried about their spinner situation, their batters weren't in great nick – Clarke, Hussey – so there were a lot of question marks hanging over their set-up, and the media were feasting on them from the moment we arrived.

We played golf on our first day, at Royal Perth. We felt it was a good way to get over the jet lag. It set the tone for what was to follow. Some pretty keen rivalries developed and a fair amount of money changed hands. It began with Collingwood and Strauss versus Anderson and Prior. There are no holds barred. If you show any sign of weakness you can expect some words coming your way. If you miss a short putt or two, then on the next green I'll be making you putt it even if it's almost a tap-in. If you're struggling with the fade and there's water on the right, the guys will let you know about the possibility of it going in the water. It's a bit of fun, but there's always an edge to it and I think that's usually the case with any professional sportsman. The competitive juices start flowing and it's win at almost all costs.

Golf is an extension of your character. Jimmy Anderson has the potential to get very moody on the golf course and once he's in that frame of mind it's quite hard, as his partner, to keep him switched on. Jonathan Trott, on numerous occasions on the tour, got us into trouble with club members with his course etiquette and language, which surprised none of us, to be honest.

Matt Prior, as with his cricket, has all the gear – tailor-made gloves, brand-new, very clean shoes, cap, sweatbands, the whole lot. He looks the part, but it has been known for him not to follow up his look with quality golf.

KP doesn't play golf. I think he was concentrating on his suntan.

Stuart Broad just wants to hit the ball as hard as he can; he doesn't mind how many shots it takes to get the ball in the hole. For him, it's an ego trip to say he can hit the ball further than anyone else. He's definitely a drive-for-show man. People might say I'm a putt-for-dough man. I'd say I'm a solid, reliable golfer and don't make many mistakes. I just take pride in winning. Collingwood and I were a reasonable partnership. We both play off four, and were giving Anderson and Prior a lot of shots. We were three down with three to play, but came back to halve it, which they didn't particularly enjoy.

We also needed to get used to cricketing conditions in Australia as soon as possible, and Perth was perfect for that. The nets at the WACA are the bounciest in world cricket, and the bowlers were asked to run in pretty much straight away so that we could get a feel for that bounce and what our shot options were. The downside of it was you had to take a few blows now and again. Graeme Swann was our first casualty, getting whacked pretty hard on the finger in our first session, trying to get behind a ball. Thankfully it wasn't broken. He made sure from then on to give himself a bit of room rather than getting behind it, which was a sensible option.

On our second day we had a full-on 'scenarios' practice session in the middle in South Perth. The idea was to imagine yourself in specific situations. So, the opening batsmen had to bat as if it was the first ten overs, while middle-order batsmen had to face a spinner and maybe a seamer at the other end. One session consisted of bumper warfare for seven or eight overs. The batsmen got a lot out of it, getting to know when to duck – and also how to get off strike when there's a lot of short balls.

It's good match practice: you're out if you're out, with fielders in appropriate positions, different people captaining each scenario, bowlers bowling four or five overs and then getting a bit of a rest. We're always trying to move away from the bog-standard net session. You get quantity in nets but not that much quality in terms of improving your game, and these scenario sessions are a good way of achieving that. We started them in the West Indies for one-day cricket, but that was the first we'd done for Test cricket. They're good because you can be made to look stupid in front of your peers. You have to have your head on and think clearly about what you want to do.

Cook and I had to bat ten overs against the new ball. We survived, but we didn't score many runs. We were something like 19 for 0. In each scenario there were about four batsmen padded up. The bowlers had to take two wickets, and if they did that, you went on to the next scenario. For the batsmen the target was 40 runs, so we drew that scenario. It was a good way to get the tour off to an energetic start – guys were diving round in the field. It engages everyone with what the cricket is going to be like in Australia.

In Perth we were able to do everything relatively anonymously. There weren't many people there, the media presence was quite small and we could keep a low profile as we tried to get our preparations as close to perfect as possible. It was so relaxed I was almost concerned we'd get a shock out of nowhere and we wouldn't be prepared for it. England sides, certainly since I'd been involved, seemed to be at their best when there was a touch of desperation – having to prove ourselves after being beaten. That's when we played well. When we played less well was when we were feeling happy and comfortable with ourselves. That was the nagging doubt I had, but I'd still far prefer us to be feeling relaxed and in control rather than out of nick and unprepared.

Stuart Broad really stood out. He was absolutely loving the extra bounce and pace in the wickets. You could tell he thought they would be perfect for his style of bowling. Also, off the pitch he was designated the golf course coordinator and he was rushing about trying to arrange rounds for us. He was really relishing being on his first Ashes tour and was full of confidence that we were going to play well. I remember him saying at one of those pre-tour dinners, 'Look, I don't have any negative feelings about playing in Australia at all. All I've done is beat Australia and I don't see any reason why we can't do it again.'

5–7 November, Perth, England XI v Western Australia

This was a really good start to the tour. Last time our first game had been a one-dayer against the Prime Minister's XI. We didn't have our one-day squad there with us so it was a rather pointless fixture and we were beaten comprehensively by a strong side. This time we went straight into a three-day game against Western Australia. They put out pretty much their full side, so it was a good, solid, competitive fixture.

We went into the game with the intention of putting into practice the things we'd learnt from the nets – not driving too early in your own innings, not hitting the ball on the up. If you can't play a cross-batted shot early, don't play anything. That was all good advice, yet we found ourselves four down pretty quickly, with the captain among those trying to force using a straight bat off the back foot.

Throughout our preparations we'd talked about the impor- tance of winning the warm-up games – in fact, of not talking about them as warm-up games, but as first-class fixtures. But at the start of the third day, a win seemed a long way off. Western Australia were 130 ahead, one wicket down in the second innings. We were facing the prospect of a long day in the field playing out a meaningless draw, or possibly even Western Australia having a session and a half to bowl us out on the final afternoon.

What followed was a very impressive spell of bowling, by Broad in particular. By the time we got two or three wickets, it felt as if they might lose a wicket every ball. When they weren't getting out they weren't scoring that easily, as they were finding it hard to deal with Broad and Finn's bounce and Swann was whirling away very effectively at the other end. Eventually we bowled them out, leaving us needing 242 in about 55 overs.

After a bit of an uncomfortable period against the new ball and the loss of Alastair Cook and Trott, Kevin Pietersen and I were able to get some momentum going, and I took the boys over the line to register England's first victory against Western Australia since the 1950s. Incidentally, England went on to win that series.

Once I got through the new ball it was about pacing the innings and making sure I was there at the end. I ended up 120 not out, and we won with about three or four overs to go, so it was a very professional performance on the last day from both batsmen and bowlers. We had a few beers in the dressing room afterwards and reflected on what we'd achieved. It's never easy to win a three-day game, but we'd managed to do it in Perth, in probably the most hostile conditions we were likely to encounter. Things were going according to plan.

I knew that as a captain I had to get runs on the tour. I think it's important to lead from the front and it's particularly important in Australia that the opening batsmen do their job and get through that new ball. The more you play for England, the more you realise that not scoring runs in warm-up games can add so much pressure that it actually becomes very difficult to bat. It was good I was not in that position.

11–13 November, Adelaide, England XI v South Australia

Before the second warm-up game, there were more nets and more golf, which was important for relaxation purposes. David Saker, the bowling coach, went and bought the 'clown of the week' suit, which was to be awarded to the person who'd made the biggest fool of himself over the course of the week. Saker himself was the first recipient. He looked hilarious; it was a Spider-Man-type outfit. The idea originally was that you had to wear it out that night, but the costume was so incredibly bad we thought it might bring the England team into disrepute. One look at Saker's body in the suit confirmed that opinion. (He won it again later by taking the roof off the minibus by not heeding the height warnings in the underground car park at the MCG – his home ground. He won it for life after that.)

The best thing about the Adelaide game was the very welcome return to form of Alastair Cook. He'd arrived on the tour under quite a lot of pressure for his place and he'd been out cheaply twice against Western Australia. So although we were confident he would come around, he was very concerned about his form and worried that any technical issues he had might be exposed by the extra bounce in Australia. He grafted incredibly hard for 32 in the first innings, batting a whole session, and then in the second made a magnificent 111.

He had definitely been anxious. You could tell in the nets he was feeling for the ball. When you're not confident, batting seems very difficult – you start thinking about it rather than reacting to the ball – and he had to dig very deep for the first half-hour in the first innings. He got a lot of thick edges, but he did what he's done throughout his career: he picked up runs. By doing that, he started feeling a bit more comfortable at the crease, and we saw the benefit of that in the second innings.

Collingwood also played very well, having missed out in Perth, so by that early stage of the tour, almost all our batsmen had got some runs. Again, we bowled the opposition side out cheaply, something we hadn't managed the last time we were there. Any similarities between this tour and the previous one were rapidly being erased.

We nailed our colours to the mast in terms of what our batting order would be. We had said that those warm-up games were firstly about winning, but also about getting the guys who were likely to play in the first Test in as good form as possible. They weren't about giving everyone in the squad a go. We felt that it was more important to make sure we got the tour off to a winning start than that everyone had a bat.

Those with a chance of coming into the side at some later stage would just have to make sure they did as much as they could in the nets to make themselves ready, though we realised it was going to be difficult for them.

It was a tough call on Eoin Morgan. He was technically the man in possession of the number five spot. We explained to him that we felt Bell and Collingwood's experience out here put them in good stead and that it was very possible that he would get an opportunity at some stage during the tour and that he should make sure he was ready to take it. Obviously, he was disappointed, but in those Australian conditions we felt that Bell's game in particular was more suited.

Towards the end of the game, we announced that we were sending our front-line bowling attack off to Brisbane, the venue for the first Test. Andy Flower had suggested it at the start of the tour, saying there wasn't a huge amount to be gained from the bowlers playing in the last warm-up game in Hobart, where the conditions were likely to be very different. It was more important for the bowlers to get used to the heat and humidity in Brisbane. That was going to be a big challenge for them.

It made a lot of sense; we didn't really want to play our first-team bowlers a week before the Test anyway. The only question was whether any of them needed more bowling than they'd got in the first two warm-up games. There was certainly a case for Steven Finn playing in that final warm-up game, but we decided he'd benefit more from the preparation time in Brisbane.

We were certain of our first-choice bowling attack by then. Finn had been a very important part of the line-up during the summer. He'd had a great start to his career and was very confident. We liked the fact that his height would allow him to get steep bounce, and he, Broad and Anderson had developed a good understanding of each other in the series. The others in the running, Ajmal Shahzad, Tim Bresnan and Chris Tremlett, hadn't had an opportunity to bowl yet on the tour. But we were very comfortable with the other three at that stage.

14–16 November, Hobart

The plans were coming together. We'd played good cricket, the batsmen had all done pretty well and so had the bowlers. We were conscious that the Australia A fixture in Hobart was going to be a big one, especially as we were without our three main seamers. We also realised that in the past, Australia A games had provided a great opportunity for young Australians to show their talent and send a signal to England sides that there were a lot more than the first XI in Australia capable of competing against the England side.

So, we went to Hobart determined to play well, and not just to keep the momentum going into the Test match. One of the points I made to the players was that at some point during the series, or in the future, members of that Australia A side would be taking part in Test matches against us. It was very important that they should have negative memories of playing against England.

We had some practice sessions and a bit of golf at Royal Hobart. It was quite relaxed. We also had a gym session in the sports centre in Hobart, which was followed by a warm-down in the pool, where there was a 10 metre diving board. It was KP who suggested it. A couple of the guys had dived from the 3 metre board and one from the 5 metre board. Then, as is always the case, someone always has to be bigger and better. It was very interesting to see which players plucked up the courage to jump off and how long it took. They didn't just walk to the end and jump – there was a whole mental-rehearsal process to go through. We were dealing with potential death, even though from the bottom it didn't look too high at all.

In the end most from the first group jumped: Collingwood, Pietersen, Prior, Cook. It was one of the most intimidating things I've ever done. You have to try everything once, but I don't think I'll do it again. It feels as if you're falling for ever, but the tricky thing is getting your head around jumping off in the first place. You're pre-programmed not to jump from that height. I have done a bungee jump, but when you're wearing a harness it's not such an issue because you know you're going to be fine. When it's just you jumping out, it's harder work.

We were all really happy with how Pietersen was doing. He'd started the tour in positive fashion against Western Australia, smacking the ball everywhere, especially in the second innings. From a guy who'd been out of form for a while it was great to see. He was back and he was playing in a way that we all knew he could. He had to dig a bit deeper in Adelaide but he got a good thirty and he had the bit between his teeth right from the start. It was something he really wanted to achieve in his life, winning the Ashes in Australia. When he'd been left out of the one-dayers against Pakistan, he could have reacted badly, but he came back in and got amongst it and relished being one of the senior players again.

He's not a big one for meetings, but he has some very good stuff to offer. He thinks a lot about the game of cricket. He was the one player who scored runs on the 2006–07 tour, so he was constantly talking about how much easier it was once you got yourself in and it was just a case of getting through those first twenty balls. It sounds obvious, but he'd actually done it last time around, which added a lot of credence to what he was saying.

I've always found Kevin pretty good to manage. He has a great work ethic and a really strong will to do well, so he sets a good example for the other players. Of course he likes to be the centre of attention and he likes to be the number one guy in the team, but I don't think that's a bad thing. As long as he's setting the right example, I think it's an admirable quality to have. Most of the best players in the world are similar.

I often have chats with him, but he's someone who generally can look after himself. He obviously found it tough when he wasn't scoring runs, but a lot of the issues that surround Kevin aren't necessarily of his own making. I think the media like to jump on anything he says in the way they did with Andrew Flintoff, because they see them as the big characters in the team and the big star players.

The Sprinkler Dance

A couple of days before the Australia A game, our sponsors Brit Insurance organised a day with the media. Our coaches were meant to put the journalists through their paces and show them some of the drills we do, and generally make as much of a fool out of them as possible, which they did very successfully. I always think it's a good thing to do some light-hearted stuff with the media, and appreciate that behind the articles, a lot of them are actually reasonable blokes and good fun.

During the day, Graeme Swann was doing some filming for his new Ashes diary and he was trying to get players to do the Sprinkler Dance. It was something that I think Paul Collingwood originated – I don't know where, in some dodgy nightclub somewhere – and a few of the lads had copied him. Jimmy Anderson and Swanny seized on it pretty quickly. Swanny thought that if he could get everyone doing the Sprinkler, and then put it to music, it would be a great way to launch his diary alongside images of the *Independent*'s Stephen Brenkley trying to stretch and warm up. I didn't really know what it entailed, so I slightly sidestepped it and just did a little jig for him. It was the start of Sprinkler mania, and from then on there were thousands of videos sent into the ECB of people doing their own versions. It really took off and became a bit of a cult. It helped to give the impression that we were relaxed and enjoying ourselves; we weren't stressed out and sheltering in our hotel rooms – we were actually having a bit of a 'craic', as the Irish put it.

That's one of the great strengths that Swann brings to our group: he's an amazingly funny bloke. I'd never say that to his face, obviously – but he sees the light-hearted side of everything. In an environment where things can get quite stressful and dispiriting, it's fantastic to have someone like that who just reminds you that the latest horrendous fielding display or shocking batting performance is not the end of the world – we'll be laughing about it in a week's time anyway. It's a great skill of his and very valuable.

17–20 November, Hobart, England XI v Australia A

We were exactly where we wanted to be. At the end of the match I specifically said that to Andy Flower, and emphasised what a big victory it was. Our second-string bowling attack had bowled them out twice and we'd beaten them by ten wickets. I was very surprised by how skilfully they bowled, having played no cricket up to that point. Tremlett looked very threatening on a wicket that wasn't particularly helpful and both Bresnan and Shahzad reversed the ball beautifully.

Bell in particular showed his class in getting 192. It included a calculated attack on Steve Smith, who came into the game with a big reputation. Bell decided to take him down right from the offset and not let him settle. It was pretty brutal. Smith ended up getting him out, but that was not before he was going at six an over and finding it very tough to bowl any dot balls.

It showed that Bell was at ease with himself and really confident in his ability. We all knew about Bell's amazing talent and technique, but at times he'd lacked the self-confidence to go after the ball. In the last twelve months he'd really turned a corner. He'd settled down and got engaged, and suddenly here was a guy who didn't feel he had so much to prove. This innings was a demonstration that he was ready to take on anybody, and it was a sign of a very mature Test match player.

Collingwood chipped in with 89 and then we bowled them out cheaply again. Chris Tremlett was really impressive. He came into the game ill, with a bit of flu, but well before the start of the game he said, 'I'm absolutely fine, I'll play,' even though the doctor said he had a pretty high temperature. I was interested to see how he'd react to that, but he ran in with real aggression the whole way through, not just for the first spell. He was also very skilful with the reverse-swinging ball, which I hadn't really expected from him at all. I expected him to hit the deck pretty hard, but over the two or three years since we'd last seen him, he'd obviously added a couple of strings to his bow. He knew what he was about as a bowler now; he knew that he was ready to play at that level.

He's definitely an intimidating bowler to face. He runs in quite fast and just gets bigger and bigger. You know that it's going to be reasonably quick, it's going to have a lot of bounce on it and there's a good chance it is going to be up in your ribcage, which is where batsmen don't want the ball – it messes up your footwork. The great thing about Tremlett is that he's accurate as well. He doesn't bowl much rubbish. A lot of bowlers of that type end up bowling short and wide and getting cut and pulled and scored off pretty quickly. Tremlett actually holds the length really well, but he's got that extra intimidation factor, which is a pretty lively combination.

He's a quiet bloke, but I think in the past he was very worried about his body. It gave up very quickly, which meant he probably didn't put quite as much into his bowling as he could have for fear of breaking down. For the last twelve months or so he had had no injury concerns and therefore he had developed a lot more confidence about running in and getting in the batsmen's face a bit more. He's not a bowler who's always snarling and sledging, that's never going to be his way, but there was a nice level of 'Okay, I mean business' about him this time.

So we were savouring our victory over Australia A with a beer in the dressing room. We all felt great. The first part of the tour had gone exactly to plan and it was just what we had talked about all those months ago. But once we boarded that flight to Brisbane for the first Test, the tour was going to enter a completely different phase. The nice, quiet, relaxed build-up was going to be transformed into a very pressurised environment. We still had to play the same cricket, but it was going to

be a far greater challenge. But for the moment our performances had sent out a very strong message. The Australians
were bound to have watched that game on television, and we
had sent out a clear signal that we were going to be a tough
nut to crack.

10

ENTERING THE GABBATTOIR

24 November 2010, Brisbane

W<small>E</small> head to the first Ashes Test in the best possible frame of mind. I do know, though, that everything we've done so far goes out of the window tomorrow. It's purely a question of which team settles fastest and plays the percentages best. I get the feeling I'm going to have a pretty difficult decision to make at the toss. It looks as if there might be some green in the wicket, which makes it tempting to have a bowl, but past history, as well as Nasser's decision a few years ago, makes that option quite unappealing. On the other hand, batting first in difficult conditions may put us out of the Test match. Horrible decision really.

All the laid-back slipping-under-the-radar atmosphere had been shattered by a huge array of news crews and photographers. The day after we arrived was a day off. A few of us decided to play golf, but even leaving the hotel on our way to the golf course we were met by a throng of photographers eager to get our comments on how we were feeling before the game. The two days' practice prior to the Test match had had a real businesslike atmosphere. It was certainly less relaxed, a bit quieter; people were trying to get their minds around what their particular job was going to be over the coming five days, as well as trying to get used to the Brisbane net surfaces. In fact, the nets seemed to be remarkably slow – none of us could really believe that the wicket in the middle was going to be the same.

We had our customary pre-series meeting, in which Nathan Leamon, our analyst, very cleverly showed us reams of data on the Australians' strengths and weaknesses, but then consolidated it down into two or three very simple tips about where to bowl to any particular batsman. These days, with Hawk-Eye footage, you can see where a batsman averages on every six-inch grid on the pitch. Some of the results are quite illuminating in terms of just how different various batsmen's strengths and weaknesses are. You can click anywhere on the pitch and see how he's got out when the ball's in that area.

Hussey was a great example. If you were on the stumps, his average was significantly lower than if you bowled fifth stump. If you bowled every ball in a six-inch grid on the stumps during his career, he would average 17.6. If you bowled short and wide at him, he'd average something like 126. But Ponting averaged much higher straight than wide, which is a bit of a surprise, because the perception is that he's vulnerable to the lbw.

We looked at some footage of their bowling too, but we

tend not to study their bowlers in quite such microscopic detail because the last thing you want is to be watching them taking loads of wickets – that doesn't plant a particularly positive image in your mind. So we just saw some footage of them bowling reasonable-length balls and being defended. And then it ended up with us chatting individually or as a batting group about what to be wary of.

The Australian selection for the first Test had become a bit of a soap opera. It amused us because it seemed so familiar from past Ashes campaigns – but with England. Not knowing what your best side is, hedging your bets, plucking someone out of obscurity to be your saviour – it was all the stuff we used to do. We found it quite funny that they named seventeen people in their squad – that demonstrated that they weren't sure who their best team was. You need to know your best side well before the first Ashes Test.

Their picking Xavier Doherty ahead of Hauritz was definitely a surprise for us. We weren't disrespecting him, but his first-class record wasn't all that great and we were all expecting Hauritz to play – he'd been part of their set-up for quite a long time, and he'd actually bowled pretty well at us in the 2009 Ashes series.

My usual routine before a Test is to try to get out after practice and have a look round the city. I went out with Colly, KP and Kirk Russell, the physio, and we had a coffee in the centre of Brisbane. We just soaked up the atmosphere, and an incredible number of people came up to us, both Australians and English, saying, 'Go well tomorrow – hope it's a great series.' I was accosted by a group of drunken Geordies telling me, 'You've got to do this. You've got to do this. Failure isn't an option.' Which wasn't particularly what I wanted to hear; I think I knew that was the case anyway.

Then it was pretty much lock-down mode from 7 p.m. onwards. Just trying to gather my thoughts together, get all my kit organised, write something in my diary, look over some footage of past innings against Australia. What you're aiming to do is to visualise as much as you can what you're likely to go through the next day. I've got a disk with all my Test centuries on it, so I was looking at the runs I'd scored against Australia in 2009 – the hundred at Lord's and some of the last innings at The Oval.

The idea is to reconnect with what you were thinking on that day. But it's also good to remind yourself that under real pressure you can go out and perform. You know it's going to be an intense atmosphere and you want to feel comfortable that it's not going to overawe you, that you'll be able to cope with it pretty well. But the day before an Ashes series still feels pretty nerve-wracking. You're worried that this might be the series when you're finally outed as a fraud and not up to playing at this level. Even though you've done it loads of times before. And that's why it's good to reconnect and remind yourself that 'Okay, I've done this – I've been there before. It's going to be fine.'

25 November, Brisbane, 1st Test, day 1

I slept really badly. I didn't drop off until about 2 a.m., and I was up again at about 5.30. Your mind plays through all the things that might happen the next day – what's the first ball going to be? What am I going to do if I win the toss? You're wondering what the gods have in store for you, and your mind's turning over all sorts of different scenarios. You imagine yourself smashing the first ball of the Ashes series for four, and then you imagine yourself being caught at first slip, and then you imagine whipping one through midwicket. So many thoughts – and not many of them particularly helpful.

It was one of the strangest wickets I've seen. The groundsman had put a lot of grass sprinkles on top of it. So it looked beautiful, but if you flicked them away, there was a good covering of green grass underneath them. There were a couple of strong reasons for choosing to bowl. The first was that if there was any green in the wicket, it was likely to be hard work for the first session before flattening out in the second half of day one and day two. The second was the atmosphere of the occasion, which might be more likely to get to batsmen than bowlers. Counter to that was the feeling that, well, those are pretty negative reasons for making a decision, and at the start of the series you have to be absolutely certain that the ball's going to do quite a lot before bowling first, otherwise you can fall flat on your face. As Nasser Hussain did in 2002.

I hadn't really spoken much to Nasser except at a question-and-answer session at Lord's the day before we left for the Ashes. Nasser was in the audience. Someone said, 'Have you asked previous captains about the challenges of winning out there?' I said, 'Well, I've asked a lot of people about how to play out there – but the one person I haven't asked is Nasser Hussain, especially when it comes down to the toss at Brisbane.' Which was a bit of a cheap shot in his direction, but everyone quite enjoyed it. Now here I was at Brisbane going through the same dilemma that he'd faced eight years before. Which was quite ironic – and probably something I deserved.

Everyone was really quiet on the bus in the morning. I said to Trotty, 'It's the biggest load of nonsense ever that a quiet bus means that we won't play well. Of course it's going to be quiet – you've got a big day ahead of you and you're trying to sort your mind out for what's coming up.' And Trotty said, 'Yeah, absolutely right.' It was a relaxed quietness, and not something that worried me at all.

As soon as I got to the ground I went out to the wicket and made my mind up that I was going to bat first. The wicket looked a little better than the day before. They'd cut it down a bit overnight, and although it was clouding over, it was still primarily sunny. I think I was probably swayed most by the idea of actually taking what I felt was a positive option. Later in the series we went against that, but at this stage – the first round of the battle – I thought it was important to grab the

the front foot against Australia in the Ashes series of 2010–11. Batting for England is a
pleasure and the captaincy a privilege I never imagined I would enjoy as a young player.

Above Paul Collingwood raises the 2010 World Twenty20 trophy, flanked by (*left to right*) Eoin Morgan, Kevin Pietersen, Stuart Broad, Graeme Swann, Luke Wright and Ryan Sidebottom. I wasn't involved, having accepted I was not suited to the format, but the success helped in the build-up to the Ashes.

Left We won the 2010 series against Pakistan but I felt our success was devalued by the allegations against (*left to right*) Mohammad Amir, captain Salman Butt and Mohammad Asif.

ormed a solid partnership with coach Andy
ower (*left*). He had the respect of the
ngland team from the start both as a man
d for his record as a Test player with
mbabwe.

Our Australian bowling guru David Saker
(*right*), with Jimmy Anderson, who both urged
me to put Ricky Ponting's side in at the MCG
on Boxing Day when we bowled them out for
98.

e winner! Andy Flower raises my hand after a boxing match with a glum-looking Chris
mlett during our exhausting but rewarding bonding trip to a cold, wet Bavarian forest.

Above The Baggy Greens are jubilant as I trudge off, with a big fat zero next to my name, after skewing a Ben Hilfenhaus delivery into Mike Hussey's hands off the third ball of the First Test.

Below Brad Haddin plays another imperious shot on his way to 136 in the First Test, proving he is a worthy successor to Adam Gilchrist as wicketkeeper-batsman in the Australia side.

Above Peter Siddle is exultant after dismissi Matt Prior for his second wicket in the hat-trick that ripped out our middle order on th very first day of the 2010 Ashes series – his 26th birthday.

Below Michael Hussey's place in the Aussie te had been the subject of great conjecture afte poor form going into the First Test but this 1 in Brisbane set the tone for a strong series for hi

Right Steven Finn achieves lift-off after claiming one of the six wickets he took in Australia's first innings in Brisbane after centuries by Hussey and Haddin had helped build a handsome lead.

Below Stuart Broad's departure from Australia with a torn muscle was a setback because he was a mainstay of our bowling attack with Anderson and Swann, but it opened the door for others.

Congratulations from Alastair Cook when I reach three figures on the way to saving the First Test. After being out for a duck in the first innings, my mood is a mix of relief and rapture.

Jonathan Trott plays an unconventional shot during the 329-run stand with Alastair Cook the second innings of First Test, which Austra failed to win from a position of strength.

Double-centurion Alastair Cook (*left*) and Jonathan Trott take the acclaim from the Brisbane crowd and the dispirited Aussie fielders after batting all day to earn a draw in the First Test.

Static English fielders and the scoreboard tell a happy story as top-order wickets tumble early
the Second Test in Adelaide, where Jimmy Anderson bowled lethally on a flat pitch.

Doug Bollinger shows his satisfaction after bowling me for one in Adelaide – I lasted three balls again – but the England batsmen amassed 600-plus total that was the platform for victory.

Graeme Swann has the Australians in a spin in the Adelaide Test, his five-wicket haul in the second innings helping us to an innings victory over them for the first time since 1986.

Left Kevin Pietersen had not a century for 20 months befor hitting a career-best Test scor of 227 in Brisbane, he and Alastair Cook taking the gam away from Australia.

Below Joy unconfined as occasional off-spinner Kevin Pietersen (*centre*) celebrates a critical breakthrough by snapping up Michael Clarke i the last over of the fourth day the Adelaide Test.

bull by the horns. Once that decision was made, I felt a lot happier and clearer about what lay ahead.

We got together for a warm-up. Everyone was dying to know what I was going to say to the guys, but it seemed to me that a team talk at that stage would have absolutely no effect on what happened that day or later in the series. In the last minutes before you go on the pitch, you're prepared already. You don't need someone to say anything dramatically inspirational or original or new. And so my words were just: 'Lads, we're ready. We're absolutely ready to go, we're well prepared, we've had a great run-up to this day – let's go out and show what we can do.' A very simple message.

We went straight from there to do a lap of the pitch just to get our heads round the atmosphere of the place. As you might expect, we were abused and booed by the majority of the crowd, but there was a huge cheer from the Barmy Army as we wandered past them. This was it, this was what we'd been spending so much time planning for, and it was incredibly exciting. The phoney war was over – time to stop talking and start playing.

25 November, Brisbane, 1st Test, day 1, 11.15 a.m.
I'm sitting in my seat in the dressing room staring into my kitbag, pads strewn halfway across the room, and I'm thinking to myself, 'Has that really just happened, or is it still part of the dream that I was having last night?' Out in the first over of the first Ashes Test match – my first Ashes Test match

as captain away from home. An occasion where as leader you're trying to show the way to everyone else. The ball was short and wide from Hilfenhaus. Adrenalin's pumping through my veins. I wanted to set the tone. I saw it, it was my favourite shot. I hit it. The ball nipped back a bit and cramped me for room, and I skewed it straight into the safe hands of Mike Hussey at gully.

I couldn't believe it. On the way back to the pavilion, all that emotion, all that adrenalin, just seeped out of my body, to be replaced by a slight feeling of dread and disbelief and more than a little embarrassment that, on the biggest stage of all, I'd fluffed my lines.

No one said anything to me. The dressing room was very quiet. The rest of the team normally look to the opening batsmen to calm their nerves, but in a lot of ways I'd added to them. Yet I felt strangely calm; I realised that these things happen in cricket. The worst thing I could do was to give the impression that I was panicking or overly concerned about that being our Steve Harmison moment. So I quietly went to the viewing area and watched Jonathan Trott and Alastair Cook get through the nervous first forty minutes of the game.

Before going out to bat I had felt a little bit rushed, and more emotional than I wanted. The build-up to a game is always very nerve-wracking and there's a lot of adrenalin, but the closer you are to going out to perform your skill, the calmer you generally get, because you've prepared yourself well, you've done it a million times, and you just slip into your routine. What threw me a little was having the anthems after the toss and before batting.

We don't often sing anthems as cricketers, but before the first Test match of a huge series, with the Barmy Army joining in, it was impossible not to become a little emotional when singing 'God Save the Queen'. It was certainly a time to feel proud about representing your country. Now, for rugby players and footballers, that's a great thing – to get your emotions stirred and steel yourself for the fight ahead – but as an opening batsman it's not what you want. When you go out to bat, you need to be cool, calm, if anything emotionless, or as emotionless as you can be. And so as I was walking out with Alastair Cook I certainly felt more emotional than I normally do, even in the first Test match of a series. I'd never use it as an excuse, but I probably needed an over or two to calm myself down, and I didn't have that luxury, having speared one to gully.

It wasn't a toss I was desperate to win. I was absolutely certain that Australia would have batted – so if we'd lost and been in the field I wasn't going to be distraught, because I thought there was still going to be a little bit in that wicket. Standing there talking to Mark Nicholas at the toss, and seeing the genuine enthusiasm and excitement on his face, a guy who'd been doing that job for quite a long time, brought home what a big occasion it was.

We were all desperate to see how the day would pan out

– not thinking about the series at that stage, just thinking about the first day and the opening skirmishes. I remember vividly the nights I stayed up to watch the first day of the Ashes series in past tours, and it is a genuinely exciting thing for both players and supporters. At the start of the series, there are no psychological holds or momentum or anything like that. There are just two sides lining up to see who wins the opening battle.

There was a bit of a jest at one stage about the Steve Harmison delivery. Jimmy was obviously going to bowl the first over, and Broady was going to be at the other end, so Broady said something along the lines of 'Well, if there is going to be a Harmy ball, at least I won't be bowling it.' But Jimmy's got so much control over the ball now, no one really thought it was going to be an issue.

Everyone seized on that Harmison ball as the reason for losing the Ashes in 2006–07, but it was just one ball. It was a poor delivery, but it had such a small bearing on what went on in the days and weeks that followed. It's understandable that in hindsight people will look back and see it as a precursor to what went on. Just as if we lost the Ashes this time around, they might go back to me getting out to the third ball of the series and say, 'Oh well, that was the start of the beginning of the end.'

25 November, Brisbane, 1st Test, day 1, evening
At 197 for 4 I was thinking that we'd done amazingly well. Cook and Trott had battled incredibly hard on a wicket that was pretty slow – a lot slower than we thought it was going

to be. There was a bit of nibble there, but it was a game of cat-and-mouse early on. It wasn't easy to score, but it wasn't necessarily easy to get people out. Then Watson came on and actually swung it a bit, which the others hadn't managed to do.

I was struck by how well Alastair Cook concentrated on his way to 67 in 168 balls. It was an outstanding effort, especially as he was still under quite a lot of pressure going into that game. It was exactly the right innings for those circumstances. Jonathan Trott did very similarly, although that was something we had come to expect from him: he gets into his bubble and just plays within himself. Kevin Pietersen showed some glimpses of real quality and looked very close to being back to his best. And Ian Bell looked as if he was ready to take centre stage – he was in great form and batted beautifully as the wicket flattened out.

So I was thinking that we'd weathered the storm, and there was no reason why we couldn't go on and get 350 or 400, which would have been a very good start to the series. But as is pretty much always the case in cricket, as soon as you start relaxing and thinking you're ahead of the game, the game comes back and bites you. Siddle produced a jaffa of a ball to get rid of Cook. He followed up with a perfect ball to Matt Prior first up – full and straight – which went right through his defences. In such a big game, with so much interest from the spectators and so much emotion, the sight of someone's stumps being flattened first ball sent a charge of electricity round the ground. I was thinking to myself, 'I hope he doesn't get this ball right to Broady, because this might well be a hat-trick.' Probably not the most positive of thoughts for a captain, but that's what was going through my mind.

The crowd was roaring as Siddle ran in, and you could almost imagine what was going through Stuart Broad's mind. 'What's he going to bowl? Is it going to be a length ball – is he going to go full-stretch? He might go double-bluff and go bouncer.' As it was, Siddle bowled the perfect delivery and hit him on the boot. Plumb as you like. An amazing way to start off the series. It was obviously devastating for us, but you could see what an incredible moment it was – one that would go down in Ashes folklore for years to come.

From then on, we were scrapping as hard as we could to get to a manageable score, and by the end of our innings reached 260. The feeling in the camp was that it hadn't been a great day, but it could have been worse. Sitting in a row along one of the walls were Stuart Broad, Matthew Prior, Andrew Strauss – all our bags next to each other – with a grand total of zero runs between the three of us, and a total of five balls faced. We had a bit of a giggle about that. Prior said, 'When I was sitting in my bed last night I didn't see *that* happening today.' But I think generally there was a feeling of relief that the first day was out of the way and the series was up and running, and we felt that there was no reason why we couldn't come back the next day.

One thing you have to do when you get a low score,

especially on an occasion like that, is to make a conscious effort in front of the others to stay very positive, and appear to brush it off. But back in my room that night it hit home, and hit quite hard. Suddenly all the negative thoughts I'd been suppressing during the day flooded into my head: 'Is this the start of a horror run of form? I'm on a pair for the second innings . . .'

I was actually very tired, so thankfully I crashed out pretty early and left those worries for another day. I didn't watch the highlights that night, that's for certain.

26 November, Brisbane, 1st Test, day 2

End of day 1: England 260, Australia 25–0

We had Australia at 140 for 5. Suddenly we felt that we were back in the game. And for me in particular, it was very reassuring to see that our bowlers had worked their way through the Australian top order in Australia. We'd done it a few times in England in 2009, but we weren't sure that we'd be able to do it in Australia. The omens from the warm-up games were good, but these were obviously different batsmen we were facing.

In the end, the way we did it was nothing dramatic. We had to work really hard to break down their opening partnership, which is a highly contrasting one, making it difficult for bowlers. Shane Watson is a very good front-foot player – drives well, goes at the ball. Simon Katich walks miles across his stumps, so by the time the bowler delivers the ball, his back foot is well outside off stump and balls that are middle and off are going behind square for two runs. He mainly plays off the back foot. They are also a right-handed/left-handed combination, and the constant adjustment that requires from the bowlers provides extra scoring opportunities for both of them. The new ball in Australia is crucial and they managed to get through that. So it was even more important to get that first wicket. We felt that Jimmy Anderson had Watson lbw, but for the first time of many during the series the ball seemed to be going just over the top of the stumps. In the end Jimmy produced an excellent delivery next ball to get rid of Watson, caught at slip. And from then on we felt very much in the ascendancy.

Ricky Ponting was caught down the leg side. We were all conscious of how important it was to get Ponting out early. In 2006 he made 190-odd in Brisbane, and in the 2009 Ashes he got a big hundred in the first innings at Cardiff. In fact, he has a reputation for doing it in most series he plays, so we knew that the initial skirmishes against him were going to be telling. In some ways it was slightly fortuitous that we got him out, although he did look a little bit scratchy, as if he was searching for form, so we always felt in the game in that innings. From then on we had an excellent period of play in which we got Katich out and Michael Clarke really struggled against our bowlers. He scored 5 off 40-odd balls, and his greatest contribution to the innings was getting us to use up one of our reviews.

He inside-edged the ball – we were all certain he had, and although we were a little concerned that Hot Spot might not pick it up, you feel that when the guy's definitely nicked it you've got to go to a review. It's one of the problems with the review system that the fine edges – the ones that Hot Spot is really there for – are often not picked up. I don't know to what extent the umpires use the stump microphone. But I think that if they'd had it fully turned up for that delivery, given that the ball didn't pass any other part of his body, they should have given that decision.

The game of cricket always comes up with ways for batsmen or bowlers to gain a little advantage. Batsmen in the past didn't walk if they nicked it, and nothing changes really – if they think they're going to get away with it, players will take that chance, on the assumption that they're still going to get the odd bad decision. One of the good things about the review system is that it happens less now than it used to. That's great for the game. But the system isn't foolproof at this stage and they need to look at ways of getting further technology involved to make it better. If you can put a man on the moon, you can find a way of finding out whether someone has edged it. By and large, I think the system has worked. And the more the players get used to it, the more they'll realise which ones to review and which not to.

I went up to Clarke and asked, 'Did you nick it?' and he said, 'I'm honestly not sure,' and if ever there's an admission of guilt, that is it, otherwise you'd be saying, 'I definitely didn't hit it.' But I don't blame him for standing at all. I've got no problems with that; it's one of the conventions of the game these days that batsmen will try to stand their ground if they can.

We got Clarke out soon afterwards, then North was caught at slip off Swann and we were in a great position in the game. We knew we needed only one more wicket before we were into the bowlers, and although Mitchell Johnson is a dangerous batsman, we certainly fancied our chances against the last three. But we couldn't find a way through Haddin and Hussey, who was under considerable pressure for his place in the side. Hussey's first ball dropped just short of second slip, but from then on he played brilliantly, against Swann in particular.

Swann is as good a bowler as anyone against left-handers, but Hussey took the game to him. It was something we were half expecting from the Aussies, but more from the right-handers than the left-handers. And the way Hussey played when he went down the wicket, whacking him over his head, and then got right back on his stumps and pulled him over midwicket, made it hard for Graeme to build any pressure. On a wicket with such a true bounce, that was a smart shot to take on against Swanny. Haddin also skipped down the pitch a couple of times and hit him over his head. So our formula of putting Swann on at one end to build pressure while rotating the seamers at the other end was really tested in that spell, particularly because as the ball gets older in Australia, the conditions for batting always improve.

We're not big sledgers. What we try to do is to produce

intensity on the field – with our body language, the way we field. The bowlers might occasionally have a little word or two with the batsmen, in particular Jimmy Anderson. With Hussey, we were all trying to remind him of his predicament – one bad innings and you're out of the side, that type of thing. But it's a minor part of the game, and perhaps too much emphasis is placed on it. We want the opposition to feel as uncomfortable as possible out there, but the more aggressive sort of abuse doesn't happen. We haven't really got anyone in our side who is particularly good at it, and I'm far from convinced that it actually makes a difference. In some cases it can fire up a batsman.

Overall, it had been a good comeback by us, but that hundred partnership had put them back in front in the game. At the end of play we realised that the new ball the next day was going to be crucial. If we could get early wickets with that new ball and keep the lead to under 80, then we would be in a good position to bat well in the second innings. I wasn't particularly concerned, because I understood that it had been a hard day for the bowlers, the first day in an Ashes series, and they weren't going to get everything right first time round. My one worry was not so much that the Australians had come out determined to take Swann on, which was fully expected, as that they'd got away with it. That might have encouraged them to do it throughout the series, which was going to put our four-man bowling attack under pressure. But there was more than enough time for Swann to play his part.

27 November, Brisbane, 1st Test, day 3, early evening

End of day 2: England 260, Australia 220–5

I was feeling hugely frustrated that things hadn't gone better for us on the third day. We had started it with great expectations: the new ball was going to bring us wickets. But our bowlers couldn't have done anything more without taking wickets. Jimmy Anderson produced an unbelievable spell of bowling that somehow went unrewarded. Well, it was rewarded, only for that reward to be taken away on review by Mike Hussey, and then there was an lbw that wasn't given out. We didn't have the opportunity to use a review on that occasion because of the Michael Clarke incident the day before, which was frustrating. But the umpire is still there to make the decision, and for me that was a plumb lbw and it should have been given out. To be fair, it was Aleem Dar, who rarely gets anything wrong.

Haddin and Hussey gradually gained control over our bowlers as the ball got older, until we were scratching our heads wondering how we were going to take a wicket at all. When you're 150 behind and they're only five wickets down, you start to think there can be only one result. Fortunately, there wasn't time to dwell on those thoughts, as things moved pretty quickly. Haddin was caught at slip off Swann, from around the wicket. And then Hussey fell shortly afterwards to Finn, who went on to mop up the tail pretty well with some short-pitched bowling.

I always think it's healthy for a side to go into their batting with some sort of momentum. Even though we were a long way behind in the game, for the last forty minutes of their innings we'd been in the ascendancy, which is an important thing as a batsman, to feel that you've got something to build on. There's nothing worse for a batsman than a wagging tail. You're frustrated and you're irritated, and it isn't great going into bat with those emotions.

So, we had the momentum, but I felt very weary – it had been a tough three days. After a long hot day in the field, going out for those final ten overs was going to be a big challenge, I knew that. I'd seen how the new ball had reacted when we'd bowled with it, and it was going to be hard work. That's the most difficult part of being a captain and an opening batsman. Right up to the end of the bowling innings, you're thinking about how to get that last wicket. And then as soon as that wicket's taken, you've got ten minutes to swap your captain's hat for your batsman's hat, put on all your batting gear and get your mind around your major job in the side, which is scoring runs at the top of the order.

I'm well conditioned to it, but the more tired you are and the more effort you've made to get the batting team out, the harder it is to switch into batting mode and be clear on what you're trying to do as a batsman. At the start of that innings I was surprised by a ball from Hilfenhaus that I should never have been surprised by. He was always going to look to bring it back and attack my stumps early on, and for some unknown reason I padded up to a ball that I should never have padded up to.

As the ball pitched, I was never going to play a shot, but as I saw it coming back, my heart was in my mouth; I was thinking, 'I'm in real trouble here.' When it struck my back leg I thought to myself, 'That's a bit high – thankfully that's a bit high.' But in that situation you're almost certain the umpire will give you out, because they generally do if you pad it away. And yet that's one of the big advantages of the DRS: the umpires think about those decisions more now, because they know they're going to be overturned if they get them wrong. Great credit to Aleem Dar – he gave it not out.

When Australia referred it, I said to Cookie, 'I think that's high – what do you think?' He thought so too, but my heart was pumping. The fact that the umpire had given it not out helped – if Hawk-Eye had shown it just clipping the top of the stumps, I still wouldn't have been given out, so I was pretty confident. But you never know until the actual review goes ahead. You see it pitch, you see it hit your pad, and you're just hoping for that last little green light to come on showing that it's missing the stumps or going over the top. And it did.

It was just the wake-up call I needed, and it switched me back into batting mode. 'Right, okay – you've had one lucky escape – make sure you don't give them another chance.' Those ten overs were hard work – I hardly played a shot. I played one off Siddle, I think, where I drove it down the ground. Other than that it was just survival. There was some awkward bounce, a little bit of nibble, and it was a case of trying not to give a chance, because we knew that if we could get through it and come out batting again the next day, things were going to be easier.

That's how it is on wickets that bounce a bit, Brisbane and Perth in particular. It's genuine hard work for ten overs – your options seem minuscule. I didn't feel I could play any shots other than a kind of nurdle round the corner, and often they had a fielder there anyway. So you feel like a sitting duck for a time because you know the percentages aren't in your favour. If you take a big drive on the up, the likelihood is it's going to go straight to slip; if you take a pull shot, there's a good chance it's going to go up in the air.

You have to get it into your head that this is the bowler's time – it isn't my time. I just have to try to get through this and hope my time will come later on. It's a question of absorbing blows, almost like being on the ropes in a boxing contest. You wait for the bell at the end of the round and then come out again and start afresh – and that's what we were able to do.

I felt brilliant and rather relieved. We knew we were still in a precarious situation in the game, but we were living to fight another day. If we'd been two or three down at the end of play, it would have been just a matter of time before Australia bowled us out.

28 November, Brisbane, 1st Test, day 4

End of day 3: England 260 & 19–0, Australia 481

I slept terribly that night. Everything just crashed down on me – the enormity of the game, the match situation, the fact that Australia had been able to build that big partnership, how hard it had felt to bat that evening, and the fact that I got a duck in the first innings. It was one of those really down times when your mind races, and you're incredibly tired, but you can't sleep.

I tossed and turned. I got up and read a book for a while, trying to take my mind off things, but I probably didn't get to sleep before 3 or 4 a.m., and I was awake again at 7 a.m. So I was going into a big day's cricket having had no sleep to speak of. I'm normally a good sleeper, but luckily I've been through that a few times in my career, and I've noticed that it has no meaningful effect on whether I can perform or not the next day. You might get really tired later in the day, but in the morning you're actually okay – if you haven't drunk a skinful, that is. So I wasn't that concerned about it, but I knew it was going to take a pretty big mental effort for me to score runs that day, and not only that, I knew it was absolutely crucial that I did so.

The wicket on that fourth day was very flat and was getting flatter, and Cookie was looking incredibly solid at the other end, so to get through to lunch unscathed – I was 80-odd not out at lunch – and feel that there was minimal threat from the Australian bowlers gave me a lot of confidence that we would save the game. I was definitely thinking that we had a great chance, because there was nothing in the wicket and there was nothing that was going to hurt us.

I had been dropped by Johnson on about 70. When you're dropped, you don't really think much about it at the time, just: 'Okay, I've just got away with that – let's move on to the next ball.' You don't think, 'Aren't I lucky?' In fact, you're more likely to think, 'I can't believe he got to that,' or 'I can't believe that didn't go two yards higher, because I hit it pretty well.' It's only afterwards, when you have time to sit down and reflect, that you think, 'That could have been curtains for me.' It was a moment of luck, but I think the shot was on against Doherty, and it was certainly not a bad option, especially when you contrast it with the one I took to get myself out in the end.

Cook and I are not massive talkers – just enough to keep each other aware of the match situation. So we might say, 'Look, we're going well. We've got to make this pay.' Every over, something like, 'Come on, let's make it pay, let's make it pay,' to try to refocus our minds on what's to come. Another good thing is that because we're similar players, the dangers for us are similar. So I can say, 'He's swinging back here – you've got to be conscious of that,' or 'It's turning out of the rough,' when often with other batsmen, what's relevant to you isn't relevant to them.

Running between the wickets is really important. It's one

of the things we always go on about – making a statement with our running. Because there's nothing more frustrating for bowlers than when you're turning a one into a two. And in order to do that you've got to know which fielders to take on. With someone like Mitchell Johnson, or Brett Lee, you're not going to take on his arm, but with others, someone like Marcus North, you have a good chance of getting back for two. So it is a question of knowing each fielder's strengths and weaknesses, but more importantly having a good understanding with your partner. We all know that the one thing you can't afford when you're running between the wickets is hesitancy. That will kill you every time.

One thing I don't like is batting with someone who is overly het up. I don't like my partner coming up to me and saying something like, 'Come on, you've got to get through this over! Think about what you're trying to do! Don't play that shot!' I hate that. I just like people saying, 'Brilliant, mate – well done. Let's go again.' And actually the majority of our players are very much like that. And I think that's an indication of what gets you to play Test cricket, because if you are too intense, that intensity can find a way of magnifying itself so that you get out in pressure situations, and therefore don't make it to Test level.

I was beginning to feel the tiredness catching up with me. I drank Red Bull at lunch – which is something I never normally do – just because I was feeling really tired. I felt very on edge after lunch, as I got through to my hundred.

And after that I found myself playing shots that I wouldn't normally play.

Reaching my hundred was a huge moment because I'd failed quite consistently in Australia the last time out, and because the match situation demanded that I stand up and deliver, especially having made nothing in the first innings. There's nothing worse for a captain than getting two low scores in a first Test. It happened in my first Test as captain in the West Indies, and I hated every moment of that.

I was incredibly satisfied at getting a hundred in those circumstances, and I think anyone who saw my celebration could tell that there was a bit of fire in my belly there. It's not something I often show, but I think it was the culmination of everything that had gone on in the three days before, the fact that I hadn't slept well, and the fact that the team needed me to go out there and lead the way, and I had managed to do that. I was determined to try to be positive, because we couldn't just try to bat out two and a bit days – we had to get a lead as well, and we had to put pressure on the Aussie bowlers, especially the spinner who was making his debut, if we wanted to make life easier for ourselves. But in the end, I didn't go on and get the telling score I should have done.

I got out shortly after lunch to one of the daftest dismissals of my career. As a batsman, a lot of things go through your mind about how to put pressure on the bowlers, but for some reason I thought that going down the wicket to Marcus North, who was bowling wide of off stump, and trying to knock him up to mid-off for a single was a good option. One of the most incredibly stupid things I've done. But these things happen, and I was left to curse it for the rest of the day.

Afterwards, everything went very much according to plan. Alastair Cook didn't follow his captain's lead – once he got his hundred he went on and on. He seemed determined to get a big score. Jonathan Trott settled to the crease brilliantly and by the end of the day we were 309 for 1.

In the England team, whenever a batsman gets a hundred or a bowler gets a five-for, we all sit down and have a beer at the end of the day to celebrate their achievement. I think it's very important – to show that people really appreciate it when you've done well. It's not something just for yourself, it's something the whole team enjoy with you. And it also gives us a chance to have a beer during a Test match, which the lads love. Fitness trainers and physiologists will say that beer might make you feel more stiff the next day, but I think that's a small price to pay for genuinely celebrating one of your team-mates' successes. I brought it in pretty much straight after I became captain. We do it in both forms of the game, just crack open a beer. Someone will raise a toast to the batsman, and it really helps build that special bond between the players.

So we had a beer at the end of the day. Graham Gooch gave a little speech. And we all sat down feeling very satisfied that we'd come back into the game, and very confident that we'd go on and get the draw the next day. People were talking about the situation in the Adelaide Test four years earlier, but we knew that the way the wicket was playing, and the fact that they didn't have Shane Warne this time, meant that a repetition was unlikely.

29 November, Brisbane, 1st Test, day 5

End of day 4: England 260 & 309-1, Australia 481

There were quite a few cases of severe pad rash in the dressing room; certainly Kevin Pietersen and Paul Collingwood both had it. I don't think any batsman has had his pads on waiting to go in for as long as KP did in that situation. At the beginning of the last day, we knew we just needed to get through the first hour – that was going to be crucial. But both Cook and Trott did that with such ease that we were soon thinking we were pretty much safe.

They were scoring reasonably quickly but they weren't taking any risks. And to see that scoreboard – 517 for 1 – was incredible, and psychologically a massive moment in the series. I honestly believe that if the boot had been on the other foot, and the opposition had done that to us, we would have been asking some serious questions about how we were ever going to get these guys out.

It was an unbelievable innings from Alastair Cook. The way he played was old-fashioned in a way. He kept his tempo the same throughout his innings, which was a great lesson for the rest of us on how to build a big innings. He played the odd big shot but it was always when the percentages were very much in his favour. He just batted and batted and batted, and the bowlers got more and more tired, and he cut them away when they got a bit wide, or he nurdled them through midwicket if they got a bit straight. It was great. To me it was someone really coming of age as a batsman, valuing being back in form and being determined to make the most of it.

Cook has a reputation for being one of the nicest guys you'll ever meet, and he is. He's a genuinely nice guy. He cares passionately about the England cricket team and he cares passionately about his team-mates. He always keeps an eye out for people who might be struggling one way or another. He gets on very well with the majority of the team. He's not a bloke that some people love and some people hate. Everyone likes him. People like that are often accused of being a bit of a soft touch, but he's got great drive and determination about him.

No one trains harder than him, and he does a lot of it out of sight – not just to be seen doing it. You hear stories about the extra bits and pieces he does at Essex. There was one time when he was up at six in the morning chopping wood at Goochy's house as a form of fitness. He's a crucial cog in the England team, because no one demonstrates more than him what our team is all about – being very professional, looking after your own game and putting the team above the individual.

Both he and Ravi Bopara have had Graham Gooch as a mentor. They're always taking the mickey out of Goochy for his little sayings. It's true that he constantly repeats things that he used to think about in his career or mistakes he'd make. He'll talk about making an innings a 'big daddy' hundred, or 'Play straight, be great' – things like that. But it rubs off on them, because they respect him enormously as a player and as a bloke, and because he's put so much into their development, they feel that they have a responsibility to pay him back.

When an opposition team get a very big score, the fielding can get ragged towards the end as the bowlers get more tired and the fielders lose concentration because they don't think a chance is coming their way. But it's not something you associate with Australia, it's not something they're known for. They're known for keeping their standards very high. And that may be more to do with the fact that they haven't gone for 500 very much in the past – certainly not 500 for 1. There were definitely signs in that game that all was not well with them. Johnson you could tell was really struggling – even when I was batting you could see him lecturing himself and practising his bowling action while walking back to his mark. As a batsman you take encouragement every time you see something like that. Sometimes you may be doing it just to kid yourself into feeling good; sometimes there may be more to it and their team is actually struggling quite a lot.

Xavier Doherty certainly had a hard time. Much as English all-rounders are always being compared with Ian Botham, there's enormous pressure on an Australian spinner to live up to what Shane Warne achieved. The simple answer is that they won't. It's very unlikely that anyone will come along who is as good as him. There's a kind of unhealthy fascination with him and a feeling that he's the answer to everything. It was always asking a lot of Xavier Doherty to come in – in his first Test match – on an unresponsive wicket and set the world on fire.

At the end of that day, for us to have survived the Test match from the position we were in, to have had the opportunity to put them back in and score a few points, to walk away from Brisbane, the Gabbattoir, their impregnable fortress, taking more from the game than Australia, was extremely motivating. Especially knowing that we were starting the next Test match very soon afterwards. We felt we had Australia in a great position to ram it home. There was also a feeling of great relief that we hadn't been blown off track in the first Test of the series. That was going to be crucial for the outcome of the series – we had seen enough signs in that game that our game plan could work in the future.

One surprise on that final day was seeing how few Australian supporters were there. It showed that they didn't think there was much prospect of Australia winning the game, but also that the England supporters was in the ascendancy, singing 'Four more to the England' and all that sort of stuff. It was so encouraging to see. None of us had had any experience of that happening in Australia before. It felt as if the locals were deserting their own team.

There was a rack of papers at breakfast the next morning.

I spotted the headline 'clueless' above a picture of Ponting. It amazed me how much their press got stuck into them. It was as scathing as anything I've ever seen in English papers. It's just not something you associate with Australia. It must have been difficult for their players to deal with. It's very helpful for the opposition, though. You feel as if you're gaining something because it makes their job as cricketers a lot harder. But on a personal level you feel some sympathy for them because you know they're trying as hard as they can and they're very proud to be representing their country. To have it shoved back in your face and be told you're useless is hard to take.

11

THE PERFECT GAME

1 December 2010, Adelaide

AFTER Brisbane we all felt as if a massive weight had been lifted off our shoulders. The series was under way – okay, we were still nil-all in the series, but we felt we were probably in front if anything. We went to Adelaide in a very buoyant mood. As soon as we arrived I bumped into Michael Vaughan and I said, 'We've got the Aussies where we want them,' and he said, 'Absolutely, mate. This game's a crucial one – nail them here.'

We'd spent quite a lot of time in Adelaide already; we knew how the wicket was going to play and we had a very settled, fit side. That was in startling contrast to Australia, who'd decided to make two changes after the first Test – Bollinger for Johnson and Harris for Hilfenhaus – which looked like a bit of a panic measure. There were certainly indications that Ponting didn't wholly agree with what the selectors were doing. Whenever there's friction in the opposition camp you can't help taking something from it and feeling that they're playing into your hands.

We had mixed feelings about Johnson's omission. He's the sort of bowler who can release a huge amount of pressure from you with a bad spell, but at the same time he can get three or four of you out in the space of twenty minutes. You're happy he's playing, in the hope that he's going to bowl badly, but then if he bowls well . . . But it was an odd thing for Australia to drop one of their senior bowlers after just one Test, so overall it gave us heart.

The practice before the match was good, although slightly curtailed by a rainstorm in the afternoon. KP had a bit of an outburst on Twitter about it, and there was a small issue over that. KP was venting his frustration and he desperately wanted to have a bat that day, but he'd overstepped the mark, so Andy and I sat down with him. It was just one of those little things that happen and shows why Twitter use needs to be carefully managed.

If you've got boundaries in place on anything – whether it's discipline, or Twitter, or staying out too late drinking – then you shouldn't shy away from those boundaries and allow people to go over them. It makes it a very simple thing – okay, maybe you did it with the best of intentions, but that's over the boundary and therefore you have to be disciplined.

We hadn't changed our mind about our four-bowler strategy. The four/five-bowler argument is one that will continue for ever, unless you have a genuine all-rounder in your side. Not one team in world cricket plays five bowlers without having an all-rounder – that's a simple fact. We've looked at this long and hard. We examined a lot of information on England teams in the past, and the statistics say that when England play five bowlers, they lose more games and they don't win any more. So the theory that it's a positive move and it's more likely to win you games doesn't stack up.

What I also struggle with on the five-bowler theory is that, yes, you have to take twenty wickets, but you also have to score more runs than the opposition. So you need to have that balance between batting and bowling, and my general feeling is that when you've got five bowlers, one of them doesn't have much impact. In Brisbane, we took early wickets and we didn't convert that, but there was also a good chance we were going to lose a wicket or two against the new ball and therefore that extra batter coming in at seven could – as Australia showed – be the difference between being bowled out for 250 and actually going on and getting 400.

The Adelaide Oval is one of my favourite grounds in the world. When we went there for the second warm-up game, I was worried that the new stand might spoil the traditional cricket ground feel. But actually with a full house I think it's an excellent stand; they've done a really good job with it. And they still have the grass bank there. Every ground should have a grass bank, it creates so much atmosphere.

The one disappointment is the dressing rooms. They're in a bit of a dungeon, so you can't see the ground, although there's a very good viewing area upstairs. I don't really like that kind of disconnection between the guys who are padding up or watching TV in the dressing room and the guys up there supporting, but it is something that happens fairly often in Australia.

3 December, Adelaide, 2nd Test, day 1, morning

We were confident that the Adelaide wicket would suit our team. There wasn't the very steep bounce that you find in Perth and Brisbane. We had played pretty well on it in the warm-up game, and it brings spin into play later. So we felt we had most bases covered. Thinking about the toss, history suggested that batting second in Adelaide wasn't a bad option. You'd have to be a very brave man not to bat first if you won the toss, but the way games usually play out in Adelaide is that most sides will get a big score in the first innings, the second team will then get a big score, and then the game quickens up at the back end. But if both sides get a big score, there's not a lot of time for the side batting third to get far enough in front to bowl out the side batting fourth. So it actually puts a lot of pressure on that third innings, because if they collapse, the side batting fourth can win; if they don't collapse, the likelihood is it's going to be a draw.

We would certainly have batted first. But when the coin went up and Ricky Ponting said he was going to bat, I wasn't the most disappointed man in the world. I felt that we were still in the game, regardless of the fact that we were in the field. We had a great opportunity ahead of us, and it was important that we didn't squander it. At least three of our batsmen were in excellent form, our bowlers had done a pretty good job so far and Australia – certainly the Australian top order – had shown signs of vulnerability.

There was not a lot I needed to say before going in to field – we were all very clear on our game plan. You accept the fact that it's likely to be hard work to bowl the opposition out on that wicket, and therefore you steel yourself for a long haul. You're thinking, 'If we can bowl them out for 350, 400, we've done a good job here. In the meantime, we're going to make it hard for them to score.' What was very encouraging was that the first ball Jimmy Anderson bowled swung quite prodigiously, and even on the flattest of wickets that means there's going to be a challenge there for the batsmen.

What followed was one of the most incredible passages of play I've been involved in. Watson and Katich are not famed as a great partnership in terms of running between the wickets. They're very edgy with each other, probably because they've had problems in the past. In the first over Watson clipped one to square leg, and there was a tight single there. If they'd both gone they'd probably have been okay, but there was that hesitation. Now, when someone like Trott throws the ball from square leg with one stump to aim at, you reckon that if he hits one in six of those, he's done well. So you don't exactly expect to see the bails come off, but on this occasion they did, and that was a big psychological blow. The last thing you want to do in Test cricket is to gift wickets away – and to do it in the first over of a game is pretty criminal. On our side, we were thinking, 'Maybe this is meant to be. Maybe this is our day. Trotty's just hit from square leg, one stump; they're four balls in, and they're one down. The ball's swinging. It's going to be hard work for Ponting coming in and then the middle order.'

Jimmy produced an absolute scorcher, first ball to Ponting. The plan was to bowl fourth stump, get the ball away from him and let him come at us. We all know that when you're searching for form, you tend to flirt with those balls a bit more. And that's what he did: the ball found the edge perfectly and Graeme Swann took a very sharp catch at second slip diving in front of me.

There was pandemonium – they were 0 for 2 in the first over of a big Test match on a flat wicket, with the captain back in the pavilion. Michael Clarke was marching to the wicket. He hadn't been in great touch up to that stage. There was a gaping opportunity there, and all the momentum was telling us that we would exploit it. There was huge pressure on the player coming in; the Australian crowd was completely silent – they were gobsmacked. People couldn't believe what they were seeing. Before long it had become 2 for 3.

Clarke wafted at a few balls. He looked as if he was trying to be very positive at a time when the swing and the new ball dictated that you should settle down for five or ten overs. But he swished at it again – another beautiful outswinger by Anderson – and was easily taken by Swann once more. Incredible.

The Aussies began to fight back then and we took drinks after an hour. In a situation like that, you're still hoping for one of those dream sessions where you bowl them out for

120, but in the back of your mind you're thinking, 'Hold on – the ball's not swinging that much any more, and the wicket's looking reasonably flat, so we've got to accept that there's likely to be a partnership at some stage, but we're still in an amazing position because they're 40 for 3 on a very flat wicket.' That thought kept us going throughout the Hussey and Watson partnership. They both played very well until lunch, and for Australia to reach the break at 94 for 3, they'd have felt they'd done a pretty good job in weathering the storm.

3 December, Adelaide, 2nd Test, day 1, afternoon

After lunch it was very much Plan A time: let's starve them of runs. The wicket's pretty good – make them play the big shot. Not attacking fields – defensive fields. Let them try to pierce the outfield, and if they're not prepared to do that, they're not going to go anywhere. It worked perfectly. Watson went for a risky drive against Anderson and was caught in the gully, and suddenly we had an end open again. North came in, under big pressure for his place, and although he got 26, he ended up wafting at one from Steven Finn to keep the momentum going.

We fielded brilliantly. The idea is that we try to make the opposition feel enveloped, so that even when they hit a good shot, it's stopped. And when there's good bowling as well, suddenly they feel they've nowhere to go. We've worked very hard on that, and if someone does a good stop, a couple of people always go up and tap him on the backside, just to let him know that he's achieved something. That's something that Richard Halsall's been very strong on us doing. People might see it as a bit superficial, but we know how important it is for us as a side to function properly, for guys to do that day in and day out. Some people say that it can't make any difference, or that it's a bit showy or even just nonsense. But if you buy into it, you recognise that it's not the tapping on the backside that's important, it's the fact that a player's done a good bit of fielding and, just like sharing a beer at the end of the day for someone who's got a hundred or a five-for, it's the rest of the team saying, 'Thanks for that, mate, you've actually just done something for us.'

Matt Prior is the fulcrum of our fielding side. He's every-where – he really buzzes around. He's a very energetic keeper; he's always offering advice to the bowlers, but he also keeps the fielders on their toes if they do a bad throw. He's in charge of our fielding unit, so during a drinks break, if he thinks something's not right in that area, or our intensity has dropped, he'll always say something. It's a role he relishes.

Collingwood took a good sharp catch off Swann to get rid of Hussey, and in the end we bowled them out for 245. Amazing. It was an incredible performance. Anderson was outstanding, not just for the new-ball wickets, but for the consistency with which he bowled throughout the innings. He backs his skills against anyone now, and he's got so many at his disposal. He can swing it away, he can bowl heavy, he can swing it back; he's a very hard guy to line up, and he brings the stumps into play, which is crucial. It was a display from a quality bowler at the peak of his powers, and so far removed from the same bowler operating four years previously.

Swann had a really good day too. He did his job brilliantly. He bowled a lot of overs in that innings, going for just two and a half an over. He allowed the seam bowlers to rotate at the other end, which was very important. He would have gained a lot of confidence out of how he bowled on that wicket. I was actually a little surprised that Australia didn't take him on as they had in Brisbane. They had the two right-handers in, and Watson hit him for one six, but other than that they mostly just blocked him. And although Hussey was still quite busy against him, even Haddin didn't really play many shots against him when he came in.

It was a tremendous performance in the field – pretty much the perfect day. Great fielding, great bowling, with a little bit of luck going our way as well. And on a wicket where there'd been scores of 400-plus in the past, we felt that we already had a 160-run head start.

Going out to bat, I was very happy with life, though slightly disappointed that we had to face one over – in that situation, you're secretly hoping that it might take just one more to bowl them out. There was even chat in the dressing room about whether we should send out the nightwatchman to face the over. But common sense prevailed and, to be honest, Cook and

I were keen to take it on anyway. I was even happier when I got a leg bye off the first ball and left Cook to face the last five!

After play I had a slight altercation with Ponting. There had been a bit of by-play between Anderson and Haddin when Australia batted. Anderson had been pretty constant in just nagging away at Haddin; he obviously frustrated him, and Haddin had a few words with me when I came off at the end. He had been the last man out for Australia, so he was frustrated that he got out, and was obviously still in batting mode. Ponting came in to back him up. He was clearly unhappy with what Jimmy had been saying to his batsman.

My feeling was that Jimmy hadn't overstepped the mark at any time; it was only what Australians have been doing for decades, and if the umpires had had a problem with it, they'd have talked to me, but up to that stage they hadn't. It made me laugh in a way, because I felt it underlined that Australia had had a terrible day, and they were frustrated by it. It certainly didn't ruffle me. I took it as a great positive for the side. They were rattled, and we had every reason to believe we could go on and get a big score. The next day was going to be pivotal in deciding the outcome of the Test match.

4 December, Adelaide, 2nd Test, day 2

End of day 1: Australia 245, England 1–0

Cricketers like to say there are two types of leave – good ones and bad ones. Mine in the first over from Doug Bollinger was certainly in the latter category. Our analyst Nathan Leamon was mortified. He said, 'Sorry, skip, I think I've done you there.' Our analysis of Bollinger had a lot of footage of Australia playing Pakistan at Headingley, and he was swinging everything away from the left-handers, but he got no swing at all in Adelaide. It was actually a misjudgement on my part, nothing to do with that footage, but it was heartening that the analyst apologised even though it wasn't his fault in the slightest.

I was really frustrated because it was a great wicket and I felt that coming off a hundred, you want to make your form pay, but it wasn't to be. Thankfully, Cook and Trott looked comfortable again right from the start. Trott should have been run out, and he was also dropped in the gully by Hussey, which I thought were clear illustrations of the difference between the teams. It's easy to say, 'Oh well, we're just a better fielding team and we practise a lot harder than them.' The fact is that when things go your way, they go your way, and when they don't, they don't. Trott got away with it, and there were a couple of half-chances that went down, but Cook and Trott rose above it and carried on from where they'd left off in Brisbane. It must have been incredibly demoralising for the Australians to see them scoring runs so freely again.

Cook was extraordinary. He seemed to slip straight back into that rhythm from Brisbane so easily, which is something a lot of batsmen find very hard to do. The reason is that in a big innings batsmen tend to go through the gears gradually until they get to 100 and then they play a lot of big shots, and batting seems very easy. Then the next time they bat they start off thinking it's going to be the same, and they play a big shot and get out. Whereas the basis of Cook's double hundred was that he didn't change tempo at any stage, so when he batted in Adelaide he just played at that same tempo again.

He left the ball brilliantly and went along serenely to his century without ever looking as if he was going to get out. The frustration of the Australian team was evident in how many times they changed their plans: every two or three overs they were trying something different. I know that feeling as a captain when you think you have to try *something*, because what you're doing at the moment isn't working. But as a batsman, if they're chopping and changing all the time, first you think, 'We're on top of them here,' and then, 'Every time they change, it's providing different opportunities for me to score.'

It was 38 degrees out there – baking hot. But it didn't affect Cookie. He never even changed his gloves. He is one of these freaks who don't sweat – I don't know why. That's one of the reasons we get him to look after the ball in the field, because he has such dry hands, which means we have the best chance of getting reverse swing.

We rattled along at three and a half an over, without taking risks. By the time KP came in, the game situation was perfectly set up for him to play positively and aggressively. Sometimes he looks very frenetic early on, and on those days it's not surprising that he makes a twenty or a thirty and gets out. His best days are when he appears very calm and comfortable and willing to take a look for a few balls, when he's not worried about letting a few go by and he gets that big extravagant leave out. That's always encouraging to see.

That's what we saw that day. KP really had his brain engaged and you could tell what he was thinking: 'Right – this is my moment to make a mark on the series.' He'd made a big hundred in Adelaide the previous time he played there, he'd batted well in the warm-up game and now he was coming in at a great position in this Test. So the stars were all aligned and it was a great opportunity that he wasn't going to miss.

You could see right from the first ball that he was very comfortable with his game. He'd batted well in Brisbane. When players are comfortable they don't feel the need to get to 20 quickly, because they assume it's going to happen anyway. It was a big moment for him. He hadn't made a century for us for eighteen months. He'd had a hard time. When he was dropped from the one-day series at the end of the summer, he went away to South Africa to try to rediscover his game, which was a brave call. A lot of people might have thought it better to have a rest and get away from cricket for a while, but he took it upon himself to go away and work at it. Even with the best players, when the going's tough, the going's tough. It doesn't matter how good you are, if you're not used to scoring runs, it really is a huge mental battle to stay in long enough to back your game plan, and not to succumb to the pressure and try to get to 20 too quickly.

It's difficult to appreciate quite how hard it is to be a batsman when you're out of form in international cricket. It's horrendous – your whole career's on the line. It's an intensely personal battle, very lonely. Although other people have been through it, if they're not going through it at the same time, they don't appreciate it with you. You're looking for solutions all the time. Is it a technical thing? Why can't I switch myself on? Why can't I just bat properly? When everyone else bats it looks so easy – how come it's so difficult for me? Or am I just not good enough? All these thoughts go through your head and there is only one way to deal with it: to battle through to a score somehow.

I've experienced it a few times myself, and whenever someone else is going through it I always try to emphasise the point that it only takes one innings. It doesn't matter how bad you feel today, you are just one innings away from feeling great about your game again. When you're out of form, you may dread every innings you play, because it's such a hard thing to get yourself up for it and know that there's that kind of potential humiliation there, but every innings is an opportunity to turn the corner, and you have to try to look at it like that.

Despite the heat, Cook and Pietersen maintained their concentration superbly. The support staff play a big part here. It's an area in which Huw Bevan, the fitness trainer, comes into his own. He's always mixing concoctions, whether you're in the field or batting. At the end of any session, he'll have a smoothie for you which is part banana, part protein replacement and part carbohydrate replacement, so it's almost like a full meal. When you're batting, or when you're bowling, in particular, you don't really feel like eating a huge amount. Mark Saxby looks after the drinks. We have a special thing called Viper, which is a salt and carbohydrate replacement drink, as well as Dioralyte, a salt replacement, and various others. So we're reasonably scientific now – and are actually becoming more so, the more we tour – about how to avoid cramps and fatigue, because it can potentially lose you a game.

We give players responsibility to know what works for them, but we try to stress that it is very, very important for them to sort it out. So someone like Matt Prior, who is prone to cramps, is very careful about what and how much he drinks: he'll be on the Viper stuff from 6 a.m. to make sure he doesn't cramp up when he's keeping. For some people it doesn't really matter what they drink, because they just don't cramp up. With others, there's a degree of trial and error about it, but the good thing is that we have so many options there now.

We have a toastie machine in the dressing room with an array of cold meats and salads, but in Adelaide in particular the food is outstanding, probably second only to Lord's, so if you're not involved in the action straight away, you usually just stick to the normal lunch and tea routines. Cookie ate a lot of bananas to keep him going that day. And KP is quite fastidious about having warm or room-temperature water so that he can get it down him. Anyway, it all worked, because KP was 85 not out at the close and Cook was 136.

5 December, Adelaide, 2nd Test, day 3

End of day 2: Australia 245, England 317–2

Kevin Pietersen went on to get his first hundred for England since March 2009 and then he converted it into a double. It was a special innings – the way he played, the fact that it was in an Ashes series again. But more than anything because he reasserted his class, which he'd been struggling to do for a while, and I think it was a massive weight off his mind. I never doubted that he would rediscover his form. We all go through ups and downs, but the best players tend to stay down for less time than others, just because they're better. I kept on thinking back to that session in Loughborough when he was so clearly head and shoulders above everyone else in dealing with the bowling machine. That sort of quality can't stay hidden for too long – it's going to come back at some stage. And when it does come back, there's a good chance that it's going to come back with a bang. And it did!

We celebrated it well in the dressing room. Paul Collingwood gave the toast because he was one of the guys who had been there throughout KP's career, so it meant more coming from someone who'd been through the ups and downs of Test cricket in the same way. They've had a few fantastic partnerships together too.

In a newspaper interview before the first Test, Shane

Warne had commented that 'KP might be the walking ego with the way he struts around, and sometimes he is unpopular with his own team-mates, and can rub people up the wrong way. He does have an attitude. But he has to be made to feel important and like he is the man. If he feels like that, he will give you everything.'

I'd say KP is a complex bloke. What you first see – the great self-confidence and belief in his ability, a bit of a swagger and strut – is not necessarily matched by what he feels deep down. You get the impression that he desperately wants to be liked, but sometimes doesn't know the right way to go about it. I have never had any issues on a personal level with KP – I've always got on with him very well and he's always put in for the team since I've been captain. And he's actually had quite a few reasons not to, given the captaincy was taken away from him and the potential for lingering resentment. He needs to be managed like anyone else, but I think he has a good heart and his work ethic is outstanding and a great example to everyone. You know you're likely to get the best out of him when you need him most. That's a great trait to have in any player – in any team.

6 December, Adelaide, 2nd Test, day 4

End of day 3: Australia 245, England 551–4

We batted on for about ten overs in the morning. We were in a quandary because we obviously wanted to give ourselves as much time as possible to bowl them out, and we were aware that bad weather was possible on the afternoon of the final day, so we had to take a number of things into consideration.

In that time, we thought we could perhaps score 100 runs very quickly, which would make it impossible for them to bat on and get far enough ahead to bowl us out if they happened to have a great day. So it felt that it was a good balance, added to the negative feeling their batsmen might have going into bat having been spanked around for ten overs, and having spent two and a bit days in the field. Of course, there's always the fear that you're going to be cursing if the rain comes when they have nine wickets down and you draw a match you should have won. In the end, we scored about 70 more runs and declared on 620.

The Australian openers got through the new ball very comfortably – as we expected them to, really. The wicket was very flat at that stage and it wasn't swinging much. But from the moment Graeme Swann came on, it looked as if there was a lot of turn and bounce, and we soon began to think that things could happen very quickly – Graeme Swann, one of the world's best spinners, on a turning wicket, with Australia facing a fairly hopeless situation.

He got Katich out reasonably quickly, and then followed that with the wicket of Ponting, who looked very uncomfortable against him. He was brilliantly taken low down by Collingwood at first slip. Then we ran into Clarke and Hussey, who frustrated us. Clarke is renowned as one of the best players of spin in the world, and the way he attacked Swann was great testament to his technique. Running down the wicket and hitting him through extra cover on a turning wicket sounds like a risky ploy, but he manages to get to the pitch every time and it looks like a low-risk option when he does it. When I do it, it feels very high-risk.

Once they got themselves in, it suddenly didn't seem to be turning as much, and we didn't look anywhere near as threatening. The forecast was for a heavy storm to come in at some stage the next day. One of the old adages in cricket is that you can't worry about the weather, so control the controllables. But you do worry about it, because it's potentially the difference between drawing and winning a Test match.

While Clarke and Hussey were still in I was growing concerned, because they didn't look like getting out. Graeme Swann had been toiling away for a long time; he was clearly tired, and I thought it might be an idea to try KP. Although he's also an off-spin bowler, he's a very different type: he's much taller, he doesn't rely on drift as much as Swanny and he gets more bounce. In the last couple of overs of the day it was worth trying, because the likelihood was that they would just see the other bowlers out.

The actual dismissal was a strange one. If it hadn't been the last over of the day, Michael Clarke almost certainly would have pulled that ball away for at least a single and probably four. But because it was the final over and he was shutting up shop, he tried to nurdle it round the corner, but it bounced a bit more than he expected and went straight to Alastair Cook. It's one of those things you try as a captain, and it's brilliant when they come off. We recognised it as a big breakthrough.

'We've got to win this game now,' I said to myself. 'If it does rain, I'll be absolutely mortified.'

7 December, Adelaide, 2nd Test, day 5
End of day 4: Australia 245 & 238–4, England 620–5 dec

The first thing I did when I woke up on that fifth morning was to open the curtains. There was a bit of hazy cloud, but to my relief it was a bright sunny day. The night before, I'd been checking every weather website I could find: a couple of apps on my iPad, the Australian Bureau of Meteorology, various other websites. Andy Flower had managed to get a radar picture which was projecting that a storm was coming in the afternoon, but afternoon can mean one o'clock or five o'clock, and we weren't sure which it was going to be.

We were going to have to do it without Stuart Broad. In the middle of a spell on the fourth day he said, 'I'm struggling here – I need to go off.' I was thinking that he might be out for the rest of the Test match, but at no stage did I think his tour was over. But as soon as we got into the changing room, it became obvious that he was in trouble. He had a huge amount of bruising in his ribcage, and medical staff were certain he had a substantial side strain, which is not something that heals quickly – ever.

It was a real shock for him, but also for all of us who'd seen how keen he was to make his mark on the Ashes series. He was distraught. He'd bowled really well up to that point without taking many wickets, and suddenly his tour was over. He had been one of our big players in recent series – identified as potentially an Ashes-winning performer. So it was a huge disappointment for him and for us. In some ways, however, I felt a bit more reassured than I might have done, because I'd seen the back-up bowlers perform so well in the Australia A game, and I thought that Tremlett in particular would fulfil his role adequately. But it was a big shock for everyone.

I was desperate to win the match. I'm a big believer that if you get out of jail as a side, when the other side has played all the cricket in the game, it gives you great spring in your step going into the next game, and it deflates the team that's put in all the hard work and got nothing out of it. The Cardiff game in 2009 was a good example of that. And I didn't want our fantastic rearguard effort in Brisbane to go to waste. But once we started play on the fifth day, we realised that there was no point in worrying about the weather now – we just had to concentrate on getting the wickets as quickly as we could, and hope that we'd have enough time.

We got off to a pretty fast start. Five or six overs in, Hussey went for a pull and top-edged Finn to mid-on. It was a very uncharacteristic shot for Hussey and the big breakthrough in the Test match, because North was in, who was always going to find life tricky against the off-spin, and we thought they had a long tail. If we could get North or Haddin out, then we had a way in. And you always think that when the wicket's turning and bouncing, it's going to be hard work for the tail to hang around for any length of time.

The support we got was a massive help. The Barmy Army were singing, 'Jingle bells, jingle bells, jingle all the way, oh what fun it is to see England win away!' It kept reverberating around the ground. Haddin and then Harris got out very quickly, and then Swann had North lbw after a review. Swann always thinks they're out, but between myself, him and Matt Prior we were starting to understand which ones were most likely to be out. We went on to complete the victory by twelve o'clock – the perfect session.

Our dressing room went mad – there was a dangerous amount of time left in the day to celebrate our victory, and we made sure we celebrated it properly. We didn't leave the dressing room until six that night. The icing on the cake was popping out at about two o'clock and seeing it absolutely bucketing down and knowing that there would have been no more play in that Test match at that stage. So we had got the timing right, and we all realised that we were going to be hard to beat from then on.

It must have been particularly dispiriting for the Aussies as they were sipping on their Diet Cokes and lime juices, trying to carry out a post-mortem of the Test match, to see the rain pouring down, knowing that if they'd batted for another hour and a half they might have been safe.

Back in the dressing room I said a few words about Stuart Broad, saying how gutted we were for him and thanking him for his contribution. It seemed so odd and unfair that in our moment of great triumph there was this terrible personal disappointment for him. Meanwhile the three lads in contention to replace him – Shahzad, Tremlett and Bresnan – had a bowl in the middle. We were already turning our attention towards the next Test match, as you have to in those circumstances. We knew that one of them was certainly going to play and it was very important that whoever played was in good rhythm.

Some time after that Collingwood in his inebriated state thought a good way to celebrate a victory was to dive on the soaking-wet tarpaulin covers all over the Adelaide Oval. He suddenly said, 'I'm going to take it on – I'm going out there!' I reminded him of the time when David Nash, the Middlesex wicketkeeper, had streaked across Lord's in a rain break thinking no one was there, only to find out later that some members of the press were up in the box. But Collingwood did it anyway. I didn't watch him. He just came back soaking wet. I thought it was one of the most pointless things I'd ever seen . . . or not seen. But it was indicative of the general happy-go-lucky mood that was in the dressing room that day – there was a lot of singing songs and general merriment.

At that stage it was the best Test match performance that England had ever produced in my experience. The perfect template for winning a Test match: bowl a team out cheaply on the first day when it swings around a bit, get a huge score yourself and then take advantage of turn at the end of the game to dismiss them again. And the fielding was unbelievable. It wasn't just the catches – people were pulling off amazing stops. I can't remember anything we did wrong in the field.

It was mentioned in the press conference that it was potentially revenge for what had happened in Adelaide four years before. That was never our motivation going into the game. We were just so focused on this particular tour, and what we needed to do to win, that what happened before was completely irrelevant. We were euphoric and enormously proud. To beat Australia by an innings on their home turf was a massive step forward, and it was going to be hard for them to recover.

12

GENTLE INTERLUDE

13 December 2010, Melbourne

THE interlude between the second Test and the third Test at Perth was quite amusing for two reasons. First, after Australia's defeat in Adelaide people started clamouring for Shane Warne to come back. He, being the ultimate showman, didn't exactly do a lot to dispel those rumours. The idea wasn't completely laughable – because Warne was still playing some cricket – but we hardly thought it would be a step forward for Australian cricket if they did call him back. The fact that he had his own show on Channel 9, and had many commercial commitments around the Ashes, meant it didn't seem probable, to say the least. Second, from the ridiculous to the even more ridiculous, in the three-day match against Victoria before the Perth Test, I took a wicket!

After Adelaide we had gone straight to Melbourne. All of us except Jimmy Anderson. It had been factored in from the start that he would be leaving the tour at that stage for a few days to be with his wife as she gave birth. It's pretty much par for the course now with international cricketers, and something that I wholeheartedly agree with. I certainly wouldn't have missed the birth of my two sons for the world. And although it's not ideal, I think it's important to have context in your life, and realise what's important and what's not, if you want to be a successful cricketer.

Some of the wives were joining us in Melbourne, and some were meeting us in Perth, so for those of us who'd been away from our families for six or seven weeks it was the best possible scenario. Win a Test match, go and catch up with your wife and your kids, and everything's rosy in the world. The only slight dampener was that we had a three-day game against Victoria. It didn't really serve any purpose other than to give the three bowlers a chance to press their claims, albeit on a very different wicket from the one we were likely to encounter in Perth.

The games before the Tests we rightly focused on as being very important. This game, however, sat in no-man's-land. The batsmen played only because we had to field eleven players. No one was jumping up and down and demanding to play – possibly with the exception of Collingwood and Prior, who hadn't had a lot of batting up to that stage in the series. The wicket was deathly slow and low, exactly the wrong sort of wicket for a three-day game. So the only memorable thing for me was taking my third first-class wicket with a vicious drifting leg-spinner which caught the first-innings centurion from Victoria, Michael Hill, completely unawares, plumb in front of middle stump, lbw.

I was cunningly bowling left-arm orthodox to the right-hander, and then the first ball the left-hander faced, I bowled a Chinaman, and he didn't know what the hell I'd just bowled, and basically got confused and thrust his pad at it, and it was dead straight! It was comedy value for everyone – they just couldn't believe it. The batsman was properly distraught. There was a lot of running around and high-fiving. My team-mates, who know that my bowling in the nets is absolutely appalling, were dumbfounded. I was just trying to lob up some runs in order to make sure they declared overnight, to set us a chaseable target the next day. They did it incredibly generously. They set us 310 in a day on a very flat wicket, and we almost screwed it up completely. We ended up six down for 211. I had to come in at number eight and bat for the last hour to save the game.

All the bowlers vying to be Broad's replacement performed really well on a desperate pitch. We hadn't completely decided on Tremlett. Bresnan came into the reckoning as well. We felt that in Perth in particular both of those two were more likely to be incisive than Ajmal Shahzad, just because of the likely conditions and bounce. But we'd picked Tremlett to be an impact player for us during the course of the Ashes, and Perth was the ideal wicket for that type of bowling, so in the end it seemed like the logical choice.

We left Melbourne in great spirits with the wives and kids in tow. Possibly feeling a little jaded for the first time in the series, because almost all the batsmen had played every warm-up game, two Test matches and a three-day game in Melbourne. So we probably hadn't had the rest that we needed between the second and third Tests. But some of the guys were just meeting up with their families, and we headed to Perth feeling very confident about our chances of beating Australia out there.

13

WACARED

15 December 2010, Perth

PERTH has a reputation for having a very quick and bouncy wicket. In the last Ashes series we played in Australia, it wasn't like that at all, so the myth that it was the fastest wicket in the world had slightly dissipated by the time the tour started. Having said that, the nets definitely are the quickest and bounciest in the world, and in the warm-up game the wicket did go through a lot more than during the 2006–07 Ashes. So we arrived in Perth thinking that we might have to make some adjustments.

As always, we split into a batting and bowling meeting before the practice, and we talked about the lessons we'd learned from the Western Australia game there. They were: 1. Don't hit balls on the up with a straight bat – if you're going to play a shot early, it's got to be a cross-batted shot rather than a straight-batted one, more of a cut than a pull; 2. Perth is a wicket on which you need to give yourself fifteen or twenty balls to get used to it before you do anything adventurous.

In the nets, the batsmen played a kind of Russian roulette. They had to spend twenty minutes facing three seamers who were eager to make their case for inclusion in the side, as well as members of the England performance squad, who were out in Perth acting as high-quality net bowlers for us, while trying to show us what they'd got. There was a big Brit Insurance sign behind the net, and every time the ball hit, it sounded as if it was travelling at 100 miles an hour.

The nature of the nets meant the odd ball would rear up from just short of a length and glance a glove on the way through, and suddenly you were doubting your technique. It's a horrible test of your resolve at a time when all you're trying to do is make yourself feel good about going in to bat in two days. But it was important to get a feel for how the ball comes off the wicket. In actual fact, the WACA is a belter of a wicket if you get in, because there's no seam movement, and once the ball's gone soft, it can be hard for the bowlers to stem the flow of runs.

In their squad for Perth the Aussies picked Phillip Hughes, to replace Katich, and Michael Beer, a left-arm spinner who had played just five first-class games. It seemed a strange choice, but by that stage we'd become accustomed to their selectors coming up with surprise decisions. There were a lot of jokes about Beer replacing Bollinger – supposedly symbolic of the Australian team going downmarket. We had played Beer in the warm-up game against Western Australia, and he'd seemed like a decent bowler, so we didn't expect him to be useless. In fact, we didn't really expect him to play – we were pretty certain that Australia would pick their four seamers, and rightly so on a wicket that doesn't do much for spin bowling.

Perth was one of the grounds in Australia for which the stats said that bowling first was a good option, so as soon as I saw that much green in the wicket I was reasonably clear in my mind that bowling first would be a decent idea the next day.

16 December, Perth, 3rd Test, day 1

We were sitting in the dressing room at the end of the day thinking normal service had resumed. Chris Tremlett had run in and caused havoc straight away, bowling Hughes in his first over. Ponting and Clarke were both caught behind – Ponting to an outstanding catch by Paul Collingwood, Clarke to a wafty defensive stroke. And although we met resistance again from Mike Hussey, who batted brilliantly and was replicating rather too well his imperious form of four years before, the other batsmen struggled with the pace and bounce in the wicket, just as touring teams tend to do.

So, at the end of the first day we were very happy: 268 all out justified our decision to bowl first – let's put it that way. The only nagging doubt I had was that four years before, we'd bowled Australia out for 250 on the first day, and that had ended up being a pretty decent score. So I wasn't totally sure how far in front we were in the game, but we were definitely cock-a-hoop at bowling them out on the first day of a Test match again.

Before the close, Cook and I also managed to weather an awkward and quite nasty session for ten overs or so. We knew that we'd got over the worst of the new ball, so things were looking very positive for the next day.

17 December, Perth, 3rd Test, day 2

End of day 1: Australia 268, England 29–0

Half an hour before lunch on the second day, things were looking even rosier. We were 78 for nought, Cookie and I were both feeling in and used to the pace of the wicket, and we were scoring quite comfortably. Then Mitchell Johnson swung one reasonably innocuously away from Alastair Cook. You expect him to swing the odd one to the left-hander from wide of the off stump, and Cookie was drawn into playing a loose shot for the first time in God knows how many hours, and was well caught low down by Hussey in the gully. Two overs later, Jonathan Trott was lbw to one swinging back, which was not something we'd counted on Johnson doing at all. Pietersen followed three balls later.

We hadn't seen any signs of Johnson swinging a ball back to the right-handers before that. We practised the angle of left-arm-over all the time, but our game plan against Johnson was to make sure that the right-handers didn't drive through extra cover, because that was dangerous with the ball angling away from them, so we were genuinely surprised that he swung it back. Trott could possibly be excused for getting out lbw. I'm not sure the people coming after him could be excused in quite the same way, because they'd seen it happen already. But the difficult thing with Mitchell Johnson is that once he gets up a head of steam, he's almost like a bowling machine – he winds up and the ball comes out and surprises you for pace. And because he has a low arm he brings the stumps into play – it doesn't often bounce over the top.

Meanwhile, having watched the horror show at one end, I managed to nick a simple forward defence from Ryan Harris at the other end, having made 52, and suddenly there were two new batsmen at the crease and we were just trying to get through to lunch, like that boxer on the ropes desperate for the safety of the bell at the end of the round. Unfortunately, this time we weren't able to do it. Collingwood got out shouldering arms, and having been 78 for nought, we were 98 for 5.

At lunch we reckoned that with a good partnership we could get within fifty runs of Australia. There was reason to think we could do so, because Australia had done it to us. But we kept haemorrhaging wickets. Prior was bounced out, Harris got a couple of wickets, Bell batted well to make 53 but was caught by Ponting at slip, then the tail-enders were dismissed quickly, leaving us at 187 all out.

We knew we'd missed a huge opportunity. At 78 for nought, we were fully expecting to recreate the scenes of the Adelaide Test and go on to get 400, 500, but suddenly Australia had conjured up an 80-run lead out of nowhere. So we were a bit shell-shocked. We knew we had to come out with the new ball and make early inroads, which we did. Finn got two early wickets: Hughes caught by Collingwood and Ponting caught by Prior. Then Clarke played on – he never looked as though he was going to be around for very long. But after that, Watson and Hussey combined in a fantastic partnership which took control of the game. They seemed to be targeting Steven Finn, and even his good balls started disappearing for four. Although Tremlett bowled magnificently throughout the day, we simply weren't able to create pressure at both ends.

18 December, Perth, 3rd Test, day 3

End of day 2: Australia 268 & 119–3, England 187

The game continued to run away from us. It was actually the one time during the series that we had to deviate from Plan A. Our policy of restricting the scoring and building pressure just wasn't working. We even recreated their bouncer theory a few times to get Smith and Haddin out, but by that time it was too late. We conceded a lead of 390. South Africa had made more than that in the fourth innings a couple of years before in Perth to win. In fact, they won easily in the end. But we realised it was going to take a special batting effort for us to get the runs. We had about an hour to bat that evening. We knew we had to have a significant opening stand and make sure that we didn't lose any early wickets.

It didn't go well. The rot started with Alastair Cook getting a slightly dubious lbw decision, which I thought was possibly a bit high. I asked him what he thought and he said, 'I think it was out,' so I said, 'Well, okay – you might as well go then!' The replay suggested it would have been given out, but it was a close thing, and once he was back in the pavilion, I was thinking, 'Why didn't we refer it? That's crazy.' I was beating myself up over that a little, but then I followed soon afterwards, nicking a defensive shot off Johnson. Pietersen and Trott were both out giving slip-catching practice, then Anderson came in as nightwatchman. Unfortunately, he and Collingwood didn't take a single that was there off the penultimate ball, and Collingwood was out to the last ball of the day. It was the kind of nightmare batting perform-ance we'd come to expect from England sides in Australia over the years – surrendering our wickets cheaply having been ground down by the opposition. Australia with their tails up were suddenly a very different proposition.

That night we were desperately disappointed as we tried to come to terms with being in the game at the start of the day and then being completely out of it. Deep down we knew that, barring something absolutely remarkable, the game was up.

19 December, Perth, 3rd Test, day 4

End of day 3: Australia 268 & 309, England 187 & 81–5

Andy Flower gave a little speech before play. He reflected on the missed run the night before that cost us Collingwood's wicket. He said, 'Jimmy messed up yesterday evening, that's okay. We all do that, but let's appreciate everything he does for us.' And he actually got quite emotional, which Andy doesn't often do. He was talking about the way Jimmy bowls, and the fact that he actually embraces the nightwatchman's role. His voice was breaking a little. It highlighted to us just how much he cares and how passionate he is about us, not only as a side but also as a group of individuals. He knew that Jimmy was feeling bad about what had happened, but felt that it was very important for him and for us to appreciate all his positive contributions to the side rather than dwell on one bad day.

The game was over quickly, but the last thing we wanted to do was panic – we had to push it out of our minds. At the time, brooding on what had happened wasn't going to help much, other than to learn the odd lesson about not assuming that one bowler is going to do one thing all the time. We just had to put it behind us. Now, in retrospect, I think we possibly talked ourselves out of batting well on that wicket. If I had my time again, I'm not sure we should have placed so much emphasis on the fact that the wicket was so different from others, because that was based on an outdated myth and we were just making it harder for ourselves.

What really hurt me was the press conference afterwards. There was a suggestion from the press that our performance had suddenly dipped because our families had joined us. We had had to field similar questions before, but I just can't understand how people can come to that conclusion. Our wives and families are with us all the time when we play in England, and there's no way they can be a distraction for us. It's something that's normal, having your family around.

What happened was that we took the decision to have a

six-week period at the start of the tour when families weren't allowed to be there, and the media jumped on it, saying 'That's good tough stuff from England because the families are divisive and the players' attention wouldn't be on the game' and so on. Absolute rubbish.

We felt quite strongly that in the first four weeks of this particular tour, we wanted to take the warm-up phase very seriously and get a lot of our planning done for the Test series: it was important that the players were all fully engaged in the process. Then it seemed to us that it wasn't ideal for the families to arrive just before the first Test, suffering from jet lag and so on, and with the second Test following so soon after the first, the same issue applied. But we had a bit of a break between the second and third Tests and that seemed to be the right time for the families to come. We also felt that by that stage the players would really get a lift from having their families around – it's a different atmosphere when you have someone there to share your thoughts with and put things into perspective.

So that's why it seemed the right thing to do to allow the families to come at that point – but then we lost in Perth, and suddenly it was very easy to say, 'The families have turned up and you've played badly, so they've obviously influenced you badly,' which couldn't be further from the truth. At that stage of a tour, they're much more a positive influence than a negative one – so it hurt me, it frustrated me immensely; it seemed like a very lazy conclusion for journalists to jump to, and a pretty inaccurate one at that.

Basically, you have switch-on times and switch-off times. So rather than sitting and watching a DVD, you're doing stuff with your family – I think that's a great way to switch off. I just can't grasp how they can be a distraction. When we won the Durban Test in 2009, two days after our wives had arrived, you didn't hear the journalists say, 'Oh – England have won this Test because their wives have come, and they're all happy and excited to be reunited with their family.' You never hear it the other way. It seems a matter of perpetuating another old myth that has long since died, and was probably never true in the first place.

14

AN EXTRAORDINARY TURNAROUND

23 December 2010, Melbourne

THE first thing we did after Perth was to have some time off. We had played continuous cricket up until then and everyone needed a rest. I had a family day at our place in Ballarat, and my parents were there too. It was good to escape from the stress of the tour briefly.

We arrived in Melbourne with our tails between our legs after being pretty badly outplayed in Perth. We knew it was going to be an immense task to turn it around and regain the initiative in the series, but during the two warm-up days, I was really concerned about the feeling in the camp. Everyone seemed lethargic and quiet and listless. I told Andy Flower that something didn't feel right, and he agreed.

I spoke to the team: 'Listen, this is our only time to prepare for the Test match, so make sure we use it – we can't have any regrets at this stage of the tour.' It's always hard to measure exactly what's going on in people's minds. Sometimes they're quiet because they've got their focused heads on and they're thinking about what they need to do, but sometimes they're quiet because they're not really at the races; they're thinking, 'Oh no, not another practice.' I wasn't completely sure, but I felt I needed to say something just in case people were cruising.

It wasn't long before I was feeling more comfortable. We had a batters' meeting in which we talked about what we were likely to encounter at the MCG and what we had learnt in Perth, and the guys seemed to have their game heads on again. It was a relief, because we knew how important that Test match was, and how crucial Boxing Day was going to be.

Everyone was talking about it being a new record attendance at the MCG – upwards of 90,000. When you're used to playing in front of 20,000, the thought of playing in front of that many can be quite intimidating, especially as the wonderful support we'd had from the Barmy Army up to that stage was likely to be drowned out by a horde of patriotic Aussies having a few drinks after Christmas. We knew we needed to keep that crowd quiet, and we knew we needed to start the game exceptionally well.

25 December

In the past, Christmas Day practice was usually very light, a bit of a joke really – cruising around with Santa hats on, a few photos for the papers and off you go. We decided to do it differently and have a completely normal practice. We didn't want to have any regrets about taking it easy on Christmas Day, so we did exactly the same practice we'd do the day before any other Test match.

We then had a marvellous Christmas lunch laid on by the Langham Hotel. It was beautiful. A lot of families were there, my parents were there, there were a lot of kids running around and Santa came. We had a table in the corner for the saddos without any family – I think they found it pretty tough, actually, but certainly for those of us with kids it was great. But as much as you want to get involved in Christmas, half an eye is always on what's to come, especially with the series tied at one-all, so it was hard to relax completely.

We were still very confident that our game plan was going to work. It had worked brilliantly in Adelaide – well enough not just to win the game but to batter Australia on their home patch. We'd also had the win against Australia A by ten wickets, where we'd absolutely dominated the game, and there was a deep in-built confidence from all the good performances over the last twelve months or so.

But in the back of your mind you couldn't help wondering if we'd just sown the seeds of our own downfall by the way we performed in Perth. Whenever I'd played against Australia before we'd always said that if you get them down, nail them, do not allow them back up, because the way they play their cricket, if they get an iota of self-belief then they find it very easy to dominate other teams. That was what was preoccupying me and certainly Andy Flower and the rest of the coaching staff. We were thinking, 'Have we allowed them back in? What sort of side are we going to encounter here?'

Reality took over. A lot of the Australians were not playing well: Ponting hadn't scored any runs; Clarke hadn't scored any runs; they'd brought Steve Smith into the side, who was completely unproven in Test cricket; Phil Hughes had come back in and hadn't got any runs. So there was a lot for us to be very positive about.

The night before the game, I was working out what to do at the toss. The stats for Melbourne were very heavily in favour of batting first, but I'd seen the wicket the day before and it looked as if it might be a bowl-first wicket. It's a tricky one when your cricketing gut feeling is saying something but all the knowledge and information points to something else, so I was trying to weigh it up in my mind.

We brought in Tim Bresnan as a replacement for Steven Finn, which was a very tough decision. Finn had been our leading wicket-taker in the series up to that point, but our overall game plan was to strangle the opposition and not give them any free runs, and although Finny had been taking wickets, he was beginning to get picked apart by the Australian top order. They saw him as a release valve in a way; as is always the case in these series, the opposition can smell someone who's short on confidence, and it felt as if Finny's confidence was getting lower and lower. So in the end it was straightforward – we knew that Tim Bresnan would bowl well in Melbourne, with his ability to reverse-swing the ball and his nagging accuracy.

26 December, Melbourne, 4th Test, day 1

Before we started the series we always knew that the Boxing Day Test would be pivotal in determining the outcome. It's the biggest event in the Australian cricketing calendar, at their spiritual home, and we knew that whatever had happened in the previous three games, the Ashes series was still likely to be alive at that stage. And so it proved.

I got to the ground early. I travelled in with the coaches, so I was there about forty-five minutes before everyone else. The first thing I did was to look at the wicket. At that stage I was probably leaning towards batting first. But, if anything, the wicket looked a little greener than the day before. Wickets tend to dry out quite significantly in the last twenty-four hours, but this one looked greener. This was a great opportunity to learn from my mistakes.

At the forefront of my mind was my decision to bat first at the Wanderers against South Africa on a wicket that looked as if it was going to do something for the first session, because I thought it was the brave thing to do and I was backing our batting. Get through the first session and we'd be in control of the game, I thought. But instead at lunch we were five down and already halfway out of the Test match.

The game has moved on from cricketing folklore, which says that if in doubt, bat. If you think there's going to be something there and you bowl, but there isn't a huge amount there after all, you haven't actually lost a lot, because not many wickets these days deteriorate massively. In the old days, I'm sure they used to deteriorate more and then it must have been hard work in the fourth innings. Now it's almost gone to the other extreme – if in doubt, bowl.

My thinking was that if we batted on this and found ourselves five or six down at lunch, it would be a lot of hard work to get back into the match. What's more, there were plenty of vulnerabilities in their batting line-up, so suddenly things were becoming clearer in my mind.

I had a chat with David Saker, who'd obviously played a great deal of cricket at the MCG. Despite initially sitting on the fence, he ended up coming out and saying, 'Look, I think we should bowl.' Then I asked Jimmy Anderson what he thought. He said, 'I think it's a bowl-first wicket.' It's very unusual for a bowler to say that: they usually don't want to put themselves under pressure. They may think it's a bowl-first wicket, but they normally say something like, 'Well, yeah, that looks like a decent wicket, we should play all right,' just in case they bowl badly. It was a really strong thing for him to say, and that finally made up my mind that we were going to bowl first if we had the choice.

It was a pretty cold day and the atmosphere in the ground wasn't quite as electric as I anticipated, but there were a lot of nerves. At the toss, it was quiet, people were still taking their seats. The coin went up and Mark Nicholas announced, 'It's a heads, England have won the toss.' I heard the Barmy Army roar, and then I said, 'I'm going to have a bowl,' and I heard them go, 'Ohhhhh.'

That was a little concerning. It's one thing making a decision for the right reasons, but you have to think through the repercussions. If your players are swayed by what the media or the crowd think of your decision, it can actually affect how well they play. Fortunately, our players had bought into the reasons for doing it and they were fine, but we walked out there feeling quite nervous, because it was still something of a calculated gamble.

Winning the toss and choosing to bowl first feels very different from losing the toss and being asked to bowl. The bowlers are under extra pressure, and the fielders are a little bit more on edge – they feel they've got to catch everything that comes their way. You think you have to have them five or six down by lunch, which you don't at all. If you get them two or three down, you've done well.

It was a bit of a nervy start. Paul Collingwood put down a difficult catch in the first over and Kevin Pietersen missed a catch in the gully a couple of overs later. Hughes went after Tremlett and it looked as if the Aussies were pumped up and determined to take us on. As yet, the wicket didn't seem to be doing a huge amount, so I was growing a bit concerned. The last thing you want is to bowl first but then lose control of the game as they score quickly, while you're scratching your head wondering how to stem the flow.

The big turning point was Tremlett getting Watson out – caught off the shoulder of his bat. Watson had been a bit of a rock for them over the last year or two, and he hadn't offered many chances to us, so to get him early was a relief, and it also exposed Ponting, which was just what we wanted.

From then on, the bowling performance was absolutely outstanding. Tremlett hit a length hard and got some decent bounce, Anderson was swinging it both ways, and Bresnan, who was under a lot of pressure to keep it tight, bowled a magnificent first spell. He got Phil Hughes out, but more than anything he kept the pressure on the Australian batsmen. You could almost see them thinking to themselves, 'How are we going to score on this wicket? It's slow, they're bowling very accurately, it's swinging, there's a bit of nibble – what do we do?'

Ponting hung around for quite a long time, but it took him a while to get off the mark. He looked edgy. We knew his injured finger wasn't right. There was almost a run-out. When the captain's giving off those vibes, it gives you a pretty good indication of how they're feeling in their camp. Then Tremlett produced a snorter of a ball to dismiss him, caught at second slip.

We'd changed our plans to Hussey. At Brisbane, he'd edged Finn's first ball – a very full delivery – just short of second slip. In Adelaide, he played and missed at very full balls. But length balls he was exceptionally good at leaving – he was the one guy in the Australian team who could leave on bounce and wasn't worried about spending time accumulating his runs. We decided to encourage him to drive the fuller ball, so there'd be a chance he'd pop one up short to cover, and it would also bring the nick into play.

It worked brilliantly. Anderson put it in exactly the right spot. For someone like Hussey, drawing him into playing the shot is the main thing, because otherwise he'll accumulate on the leg side, and suddenly he'll be on 20 or 30 and your chance has gone. But the bowler has to get it in the right spot. There's such a small margin between a length ball that he can leave and a genuine half-volley that even a number eleven can hit for four. So it was a great piece of bowling to put the ball precisely in between those and lure Hussey into an early drive, which he edged behind. He was walking back to the pavilion for 8.

Suddenly the game was promising to turn into something really special. It all happened so quickly. It was one of those spells when you genuinely felt that every time they played a shot, it was going to get caught at slip. It felt as if we had an irresistible momentum behind us that just couldn't be checked, certainly not by the Australian lower order.

Anderson soon accounted for Smith and Clarke, then Haddin decided to try to blast his way out of the predicament and edged a ball from Bresnan to first slip, Johnson was caught on the drive shortly afterwards, following up his heroics at Perth with a duck.

They were 77 for 8, so we were in with a chance of bowling them out for 100. At the back of your mind, there's always the thought that there might be some sort of partnership that'll take them beyond that, and Siddle had been a bit of a thorn in our side in Perth. But he was caught behind a few overs later, then Hilfenhaus got an edge and suddenly Australia were all out for 98.

It was a genuine shock that we had actually bowled them out for under 100 on Boxing Day at the MCG. It was certainly a wicket on which you needed a little bit of luck early on, but if Australia had made it through to lunch three down they would probably have been in a position to get 300. It's interesting that they were all caught behind the wicket. For me that was an indication of excellent bowling. It was one of those days when the ball didn't actually pass the bat that often, but when it did go off the wicket it caught the edge, and our catching behind the wicket was very good.

It was mind-blowing, really. The amazing thing was how quiet the crowd were. I ran off the pitch to the changing room to prepare to bat, and Kevin Pietersen came and stood next to me and said, 'We're one good batting performance from retaining the Ashes.' And I said, 'Absolutely, mate – if we get stuck in, we're there.'

It's a slightly strange feeling to go in as an opening batsman having just bowled out the other team so cheaply. All you've seen for the last three hours is how not to play on that wicket, but it doesn't mean *you* know how to play on it. It looked very difficult; it seemed to be very hard to score runs and it was nibbling around.

So as we were walking out to bat, Cookie and I agreed what to do: try to keep scoring – even if it's only singles, get as many singles as we can. If it's hard to drive and play the boundary shots, then just be really busy. And that's what we did. We got quite a few singles early on, they bowled some short stuff that got us off to a bit of a start, and then the wicket died down. Fifteen overs into the innings, we were 50-odd for none. You could see their bowlers wondering how on earth they had been bowled out for 98.

Siddle ran in and bowled very well, but Johnson couldn't find a length. You could see Ponting was exasperated; he'd watched our bowlers make it look impossible for anyone to get a boundary, and suddenly Johnson was bowling either full and straight or short and wide, and he was going at five an over. You look for little signs like that. It was very quiet – not just on the field, but in the crowd. You could see people shuffling out of the MCG in embarrassment as much as anything.

The Barmy Army grew louder and louder, and by the end of the day we were 157 without loss, nine-tenths of the way to winning the Test match and retaining the Ashes. An amazing day of cricket. The lads were saying that if Carlsberg did Boxing Days, that would probably be it – you couldn't have asked for anything better. We only learnt later that it was the most one-sided first day of Test cricket in the game's history. By the end of it we'd broken the back of the Australian team.

I called the lads together and said, 'Look, there can be no patting ourselves on the backside yet. This is our chance to nail them and retain the Ashes. We can pat ourselves on the backside when we finish this game off, but for the next four days we are going to do everything we possibly can to make sure these guys don't get off the floor. We've got them on the ground – they're almost dead and buried, let's make sure they can't get up.'

I was preaching to the converted, because everybody was feeling the same. It was one of those very rare moments when a team are all in tune with each other – everyone was confident, everyone knew what they needed to do. It was going to take something absolutely outstanding from one of their cricketers to reverse that momentum.

27–28 December, Melbourne, 4th Test, days 2 and 3

End of day 1: Australia 98, England 157–0

Alastair Cook and I had set the platform the day before, but we were both out pretty early on the second day. We needed someone to go on and get a really sizeable score. I was still confident; I knew the wicket was good.

KP came in and played positively and aggressively while Trott went along almost unnoticed. If you let Trott get in, it takes something pretty special to get him out. Once he's on 20 or 30, he's a hard guy to bowl at. He's so clear about his game plan that it's very rare to see him swish at a wide one or fall over a straight one. He was an immense figure of stability for us throughout the whole series. Number three in Australia is not an easy position to bat – I got out very early a couple of times, yet he was able to soak up the pressure.

When there's pressure on, a lot of English players in my experience adopt an attitude of 'It's either you or me', and play more shots than usual, taking more risks. Sometimes it comes off and sometimes it doesn't. But Trott manages his emotions very well and sticks to what he loves doing, which is batting. Australia found it very tough to bowl at him throughout the series. They never really came up with a plan that worked against him and they ended up trying too many different things. They'd go straight for a few overs, then wide, then straight again. Probably because he gave no indication of being lured into any of their traps, they felt more and more pressure to change their tactics. That's a sign of exceptional batting.

In that innings, he also found great support from Matt Prior. We weren't in an unassailable position when he came in, 286 for 5. Obviously it was a useful lead on that wicket, but we still didn't have the Australians dead and buried. Bell and Collingwood had both been out hooking in the space of about ten minutes, but Prior played brilliantly – he has a really strong counter-attacking type of game which puts opposition teams under pressure. I remember playing against him in the summer for Middlesex when he got a hundred for Sussex and I was captaining the side. He's a really tough guy to captain against, especially when he's with the tail, because he can hit the ball in some odd areas and keep getting boundaries even with sweepers out. This was a very important innings for him. He was forthright and he never looked in any trouble. We passed various milestones – 200 lead, 300 lead – and by the time we were all out at the end of the third morning for 513, our victory was just a matter of time.

All through the innings, we tried to give the batsmen continuous encouragement and support. The MCG is actually quite a hard place for the players to stay together. Some were watching from the viewing gallery, which is about 400 steps away from the dressing room, and others were down there watching it on TV. We had talked about not drifting too far apart during the game by making sure that the bowlers, once they had done their work and had a bit of a rest, went up to the viewing gallery to show the lads in the middle that there was plenty of support for them.

We took the field after lunch. The key was going to be getting the ball reversing rather than relying on the seam movement of the first innings. The pitch was now quite cracked and abrasive. The third delivery from Jimmy Anderson scuffed a piece out of the ball on pitching and that was a good sign. By the eleventh over it was starting to reverse-swing.

Watson running Hughes out was a pretty good start for us. What struck me about that was that Prior took the ball in front of the stumps and Hughes was out by half an inch, but Hilfenhaus took the ball behind the stumps when Trott was batting and he was in by two inches. A small detail perhaps, but when Australia were dominating world cricket, everyone commented that they always did the little things better. They used to be the benchmark; now we were fielding better than them, our attention to detail was better than theirs, and the nuts and bolts of our bowling and batting were working.

There was no reason to expect them to come back at us, because we were making life very difficult for them.

Australia couldn't hope to bat for two and a half days – they had to try to get ahead of us somehow. They were facing the situation that we'd been through four years before, where you need to score runs in order to get ahead in the game, but the bowling is so accurate that it's very hard to do so. You have to take a lot of risks.

We had the best of the conditions, it's true. They batted when it nipped around a bit, we batted when it was flat, then they batted when the ball started reversing. But you have to give our bowlers and fielders credit for looking after the ball well and utilising the conditions. The wicket was getting slow and low, so we didn't need a lot of slip fielders; we could have a lot of men in front of the bat, especially given the situation in the game.

The art of reverse swing was a central part of our preparation for the tour. We needed to be very clear on how we were going to get the ball reversing. We'd become pretty good at it over the last couple of years, but the last time round in Australia we'd struggled to get any meaningful reverse. So we made it a priority for us as a side that if the ball stopped swinging conventionally, even it was only the fourth over of an innings, we were going to try to get it reversing as soon as possible after that.

In Australia there are certain phases of play: first the new ball, then a flat period that does nothing for the bowlers, then reverse swing, then flat again, and then it's a new ball. If we could minimise those flat periods as much as possible, we'd give ourselves the best chance of taking wickets. So we stuck with the formula that had worked very well for us in England, which was that apart from Matt Prior, the only two guys to touch the ball were Alastair Cook and Jimmy Anderson. No one else was to shine the ball or do anything other than get it back to them.

The simple physics behind reverse swing are that if you can get one side dry and very flappy, it creates a different air pressure, which allows the ball to reverse – that is, to swing away from where you would conventionally expect. There are various methods of getting those flaps on the ball: illegally, you can use a bottle top, you can scratch it – or, legally, you can let the wicket do it, as we do. You can't actually do anything underhand, of course, because there are twenty-seven cameras at a Test match ground, and the likelihood is you'll get caught. In any case, that's not even an option for us, so we just try to make the most of the ground conditions.

There are a lot of occasions when it's impossible to get the ball reversing: if it's a lush green outfield, or the pitch is grassy and smooth. If the wicket's not abrasive, you're going to struggle – it doesn't matter what you do to the ball. But in the game against Victoria on that ground we'd got it reversing very quickly, and we knew that the MCG is famous for reverse swing. David Saker had no doubt that it's a big reverse swing ground, always has been.

In hot, humid conditions, moist, sweaty hands make the dry side of the ball damp. So we're very obsessive about keeping that side dry, and we buff up the other side as normal. If you look after the ball well enough, eventually it will start to do something. The fielders know that even when throwing it in from the boundary, the last thing you want to do is land it on a lush piece of green grass. Once we've got it reversing, we want the ball to be thrown to the keeper on the full at all times, or onto the pitch. One bad throw into the green grass can jeopardise it, and if someone does that, he gets shouted at by Matt Prior. Once all eleven of you are clued in, it's amazing how protective you become of it.

Ponting struggled and was out for a scratchy 20. You could see that he'd had a very difficult four weeks. In the past, the one thing you could be sure of with Ricky Ponting was that he was going to make runs at some stage during a series, and his record supports that. So he was as shocked as anyone that he wasn't, and that Australia were losing as well. He also had an injured finger, and anyone who's tried playing cricket with an injury like that knows it's mentally very draining. You're not sure what shots you can play and batting doesn't feel at all comfortable. So it was obviously a very tough match for him.

But there's no time for personal sentiment. There was a temptation to feel some sympathy for him, because I'd been there – not as a captain, but as a player four years before – and I'd seen how hard it was for Flintoff as captain. But whenever I was tempted, I always thought back to how much pain he's inflicted on English sides over the years, both as captain and as batsman, and reminded myself that I shouldn't feel guilty about having our time in the sun at his expense.

We chipped away at the rest of their batting with great persistence. They were just about strokeless, in direct contrast to their efforts in the first innings. It was as if the wickets were falling in slow motion, but by the end of the third day we were almost there.

29 December, Melbourne, 4th Test, day 4

End of day 3: Australia 98 & 169–6, England 513

The task facing us that morning seemed straightforward enough – at 169 for 6, Australia were 246 behind, and Ryan Harris was unlikely to bat because of an ankle injury. When Mitchell Johnson was bowled by Tremlett in the second over of the day it looked as if we would soon have the game wrapped up, but then Brad Haddin and Peter Siddle frustrated us for 16 infuriating overs with a partnership of 86. It was not until Siddle and Hilfenhaus were both caught within two overs that we were finally able to let go and appreciate exactly what we'd achieved. We had not only won by an innings for the second time in the series, but we had retained the Ashes in Australia – the holy grail.

After performing the Sprinkler Dance on the field in front of the Barmy Army and relishing every moment of the celebrations with family and team-mates in the dressing rooms, we eventually left the MCG at sevenish. The ECB had arranged a bit of a party. When you have young lads in the team, the stupid drinks start to come out – Jägerbombs and all sorts. For those us who have two kids and have to get up early in the morning, it's a horrendous thought drinking those things. But I bravely did it anyway. There were cigars and champagne everywhere. After the party we headed into the Como Hotel for more of the same. Eoin Morgan was brandishing a bottle of Jägermeister and encouraging others to get it down their necks. We were there for a couple of hours and then some of the lads went out, while others stayed in the hotel bar. We had a good eight or nine hours together as a group, which was very special.

15

NEW YEAR'S RESOLUTION

1 January 2011, Sydney

I WOKE up on New Year's Day and looked out from the balcony of our apartment in Star City, a big casino complex in Sydney. I could see the Harbour Bridge glistening in the sunlight, a very marked contrast to the night before when I'd watched the fireworks exploding from the same balcony. It was a genuinely Happy New Year, having retained the Ashes already, but it had been a fairly sober evening for two reasons: first, we were practising the next morning in preparation for the final Test match, and second, it was a corporate celebration with our sponsors, Brit Insurance, at the Flying Fish restaurant – a beautiful place with a great view of Sydney Harbour.

The England team had had an outstanding twelve months, winning every series in England, winning the one-dayers and drawing the Test series in South Africa, and winning the Ashes. Not forgetting the World Twenty20. If there's ever been a better year for English cricket, I certainly can't remember it.

I was very proud of what we'd achieved as a side. Looking forward to the next twelve months, I was thinking that there was no reason why we couldn't go on and perform even better. Winning is a habit, and over those twelve months we'd acquired the habit consistently in all forms of the game.

How do you get that habit? Hard work helps. So does having a clear game plan, but you obviously have to have good players in the first place – players who are confident in their own ability, who know what they are doing, who are able to ask serious questions of the opposition. With all the will in the world, if you don't have players who are capable of putting in world-class performances, you're not going to win.

I'm very fortunate to be able to captain a side full of such talent. There are many occasions when talented teams don't win – when the set-up is bad, when there are conflicts within the side. But you very rarely see instances of untalented sides winning consistently, because it's just impossible. So, we're lucky with our players, we have some good characters in our side, and that bodes very well for the future.

In international cricket, especially with the schedules we have, you can never afford to look back too much, because there's always a game around the corner, whether it's the final Test match of an Ashes series, a one-day series or the World Cup. There is a time to sit down and reminisce about what you've achieved, but that time is not when you have another game in a few days.

When I took over the side, I had a team meeting and asked, 'What are our goals for this England side?' The obvious goal is to reach number one in the world, but there's something else, too – to be the best England team ever. No England side has been number one in the world for any extended length of time. English cricket is very caught up with the Ashes – and rightly so, because it's an amazing contest – but, as we saw in 2005, if that is your end goal, then once you win that one series, where do you go from there? So it's great to have that as a sort of mantra for the side – to be the best England team ever – because it means that every series you play has context. Each series is a step along the path to where you're trying to get to.

Our situation in Sydney was that, yes, we wanted to be number one in the world, but we had come out to Australia to win the Ashes, to win the series, and we hadn't achieved that yet. We'd *retained* the Ashes, but we hadn't won the series. Given that we'd beaten Australia by an innings twice, every single one of us felt that it would be an absolute travesty if we didn't go on and win the series from there. So there was no lack of motivation in the side.

I often worry with England sides that when we're feeling a bit comfortable and happy with ourselves, it can be a bit of a danger time. But on this occasion in Sydney I didn't see it. I saw a lot of guys who were confident in the way they'd been playing, and determined to finish the series in style. I was very reassured by the way they were approaching things in the nets, with a quiet confidence, allied to a sort of inner drive. That's a great recipe for success.

I first met Ruth in Sydney, and being back here with her and the kids, I can reflect on what's happened over the ten or eleven years since then. There are so many familiar places and people around Sydney that take me back to a time when I was playing in the Middlesex side, a million miles away from playing for England, and battling to justify my place in the Mosman First XI. It's incredible to think of the journey that I've been on as a cricketer, and I'm sure if anyone had told me then that I would go on and play as much for England, and actually captain the side, I wouldn't have believed them myself. Certainly no one else would have believed them.

You know that saying 'Behind every successful man is a great woman'? With me that's certainly the case. Everyone sees what happens with the England team. What people don't see is the stuff away from the pitch – the difficult balancing act that we have as a couple and as parents to our kids, to try to bring them up in as normal a way as possible, the genuinely tough job that Ruth has looking after them on her own for long periods every year. It's very hard for her and the kids when I'm out of form or preoccupied with things that are going on with the England team.

I matured quickly as a person after meeting her. Ruth's a little older than me, and because to begin with we had to manage a semi-long-distance relationship, it was a question of either getting serious quite quickly or going our separate ways. We obviously chose the former route. It was exactly what I needed. Ruth was an amazing influence in that respect.

These days Ruth and I don't discuss cricket at home: home is a sanctuary from everything that's going on on the cricket field. Having two young kids is a great way of getting away from the game. And, as Ruth constantly reminds me, it reminds you of what is important in life. Winning the Ashes is amazing, and from a career point of view is something that will live with me for ever, but it's not genuinely important. What really matters is bringing up your kids and having a healthy and happy life.

On New Year's Day we visited some mates of ours in Mosman, a suburb of Sydney. We lived there for two six-month periods and made some really good friends, including New South Wales's Warwick Adlam and Ireland's Trent Johnston. We went over to the Adlams' and spent some time with them and their kids, reconnecting with the past. There were some old photos of me – drunken photos of nights out after games and my twenty-fifth birthday. It just takes you back to a completely different part of your life, which you tend to forget about, especially when you're in this England international bubble. It allows you to think back to the steps you've taken on the way to playing inter-national cricket.

If I had to make a New Year's resolution it would be: 'Make sure you really appreciate what you're going through now, because if you don't appreciate the good times, then what are you playing the game for?' I think all of us who were involved in the Ashes series knew that we were part of something very special.

16

FINISHING THE JOB

2 January 2011, Sydney

I WAS feeling very relaxed and comfortable and happy. We'd achieved the goal of retaining the Ashes, but up until then, it'd been an incredibly hard series to play in as a captain. There was all the planning, then keeping a careful eye on how other people were handling the pressure, the expectations and the tough cricket away from home, while at the same trying to keep my own game in order and make sure I was giving myself enough time to recharge my batteries. Brisbane, Adelaide, Perth, Melbourne – mentally, all incredibly tough games for me as a player and as a captain. Thankfully we won two of them easily, but they were still very hard work as far as managing myself was concerned.

I've always been quite good at compartmentalising. So there's captain's time, and when I'm in the nets it's batting time, and the same applies when I'm in the middle. But the nets in Australia aren't necessarily great confidence-building nets, with England's best fast bowlers steaming in at you, and up till Melbourne, I just hadn't felt completely at ease with my batting. The second innings in Brisbane I played well enough, felt pretty fluent. In Adelaide I only had the one innings. In Perth I got a fifty in the first innings but I didn't feel in brilliant form. In Melbourne against the new ball was probably the best time; I felt pretty comfortable in Melbourne. So by Sydney, I was actually feeling in pretty good nick for the first time.

Generally, I had a great sense of relief and at times it was as if I was walking on a cloud. We'd put in so much time and effort, and now we knew we were going back to Heathrow with those Ashes. But I was also determined that, now that we were in that position, we should finish it off properly and really make it a party and a celebration.

The news from the Australian camp was that Ponting had been ruled out with his broken finger and Michael Clarke had been named captain. When a team has lost a series and they're missing a couple of senior players, they can take the attitude that it's a fresh start, there's nothing to lose, so let's go out and show everyone what we can do. For this reason, I was half-expecting Australia to play with a bit more fluency and to be prepared to take on our bowlers more than they had done so far. But I also knew that the disruption could work in our favour. A lot of their batsmen were still really struggling for form – Clarke, Hughes, Smith.

The day before the Test we went to the prime minister's residence. Both sets of players were there. I went up to Ricky Ponting and said, 'I hear you're not playing – hard lines.' And he looked genuinely distraught that he wasn't able to take part. He said, 'Oh well, you know – shit happens,' but you could see on his face that he desperately wanted to play in that final Test and prove a point to people. It was a great indicator of why he'd remained at the top of the game so long, because he's driven – he's so driven. Even when they'd lost, he wanted to be out there leading the side back into some sort of form before the one-dayers and the World Cup. Some English players in the past might have been secretly relieved to have a broken finger when they're out of form. That's just not the way Ricky Ponting ticks.

In our team, there was a question mark over Paul Collingwood's form. We felt that retirement might be round the corner and there was certainly a case for Eoin Morgan coming in. We stuck with Collingwood because we'd been winning, and he'd been contributing. He hadn't scored a lot of runs, but he'd been brilliant in the field, and he'd actually bowled well. He'd given a hell of a lot to English cricket. We didn't know what was going to happen afterwards, but he deserved to play in the final Test match of the series.

He was desperately frustrated with the way he was performing. I know how it feels when you're out of form and everyone else is playing well: it actually makes you feel worse about yourself. 'Hold on,' you think, 'how come I can't get a run, but everyone else is smacking it all over the place?' When everyone else is out of form too, in some ways it's a bit of a relief, because at least there's safety in numbers. But I was absolutely sure that he would go out and try to play positively, because that's the way he's always reacted when he's been out of form in the past, and for him it's the right way to go.

3 January, Sydney, 5th Test, day 1

I didn't have to say much on the morning of the match. I did mention that we deserved to win the series, and that we needed to win this game in order to do so. Nothing particularly inspirational! There was a green tinge to the wicket. After what happened in Melbourne, it seemed a pretty easy decision to bowl if we won the toss. Their batsmen were under pressure – so get them back in there and ask some more questions of them.

For Australia it was much more of a quandary. They had a new captain and it was a big challenge for Michael Clarke to raise his side after they'd just been defeated comprehensively – and he was not in great form himself. He'd captained a reasonable amount against us before in the one-dayers in England in 2009, and he did a pretty good job there. We were expecting him to do a couple of things slightly differently to Ponting. He seemed likely to be the sort of captain who would tinker and try things. But when you're winning and settled and stable, you're prepared to take whatever comes your way.

I think he was in two minds at the toss, but he opted for the Australian way of taking it on and batting first. You can understand him doing that, but it did bring us into the game straight away. I thought we had a good chance of bowling them out reasonably cheaply in that first innings.

In fact, their openers batted really well in the morning, because the ball was doing quite a lot and scoring was difficult. They got stuck in. Hughes played our seamers very well, but was out last ball before lunch. Watson had been getting under our skin all series. He's a tough guy to bowl at and can hit the ball incredibly hard. If you drop short, he's savage with the pull shot, and he's a very strong driver. There are not many weaknesses in his game.

I had always thought that at some stage he was likely to be exposed at the top of the order, given that he goes quite hard at the ball, but he left the ball really well all series, and we found it very hard to get him out early. Happily for us, he seemed to have a bit of a mental block, and kept getting out when he'd reached 50. We made sure to remind him about that, and about his running between the wickets. But he's turned into a very high-quality opener in all forms of the game.

After lunch our persistence slowly paid off. We were helped by seeing a man coming out at number three for Australia who was making his debut, rather than playing his 150th Test. All credit to Usman Khawaja – he came out firing. The first ball he clipped off his legs, and then he whacked one through midwicket. He pulled one heavily from Tremlett early on as well. We'd seen him in the Australia A game. For me he's the standout player of the next generation – it's just the way he shapes up. His record is very good in first-class cricket; he averages over 50.

Fortunately, Khawaja got out for 37. We brought the square leg up, and he went for the sweep and top-edged it to a waiting Trott. Swann's a hard man to sweep and it's quite easy for me to imagine how left-handers feel against him. When the ball's turning away from the bat, people far too often have that sweep man back. Why give them an easy single? Just keep them up – force them to play a shot they don't want to.

It was the last ball before tea, as it turned out. Then it rained. They were 134 for 4 at the close.

4 January, Sydney, 5th Test, day 2
End of day 1: Australia 134–4

Normal service was resumed and we chipped away at the Australian middle order with high-class swing and seam-bowling, led by Anderson. This time we got Hussey reasonably cheaply. Collingwood bowled him off the edge with the last delivery with the old ball. Within five overs they were 189 for 8. Then the tail wagged.

It was a frustrating period of play. When tail-enders go out and swing at the ball orthodox fielding positions can become redundant. If they're swinging at it hard, the likelihood is that the ball will fly over the head of second or third slip, and bowlers find it difficult to maintain their length, because a couple of those are likely to go out of the park. You can be torn between thinking, 'We'll bowl exactly the same way, and if you're good enough to whack it over our heads, fine,' and 'Okay, you're going to take on the shot anyway, so why don't we just have fielders out, and hopefully you'll hit it to one of them.' That was certainly the way we went with Johnson, but he kept avoiding the fielders and ended up with 53, and to rub it in, Hilfenhaus, far from the world's best batsman, started connecting as well.

The one reassuring thing was that if Hilfenhaus was timing the ball, the wicket must have flattened out quite a lot. Generally, every time the opposition tail had wagged in the past, it had been a prelude to a very good batting performance from us. In Durban against South Africa we'd had a similar situation. Their tail got a lot more than we wanted them to, but then we went out and made 574 ourselves. So when you look at it rationally, it's not necessarily a bad sign, but at the time it's very irritating.

I took my frustration out on their bowlers. I was looking to play some shots; I wasn't looking to leave. In Hilfenhaus's second over he bowled me a bouncer, which I paddled for four, and then he bowled me another, which I smashed through square leg. It's always reassuring as a batsman to know you can play your back-foot shots, even against a new ball. It allows you to target the ones that they drop down short, and I duly hooked Hilfenhaus for six over square leg a few overs later.

Clarke certainly did things differently to Ponting. He opened the bowling with Mitchell Johnson, which had some merit in it. But I had found it easy to score off Johnson throughout the whole series, so it played into my hands. I raced to 50 off 49 balls and by that stage we had great momentum, with Alastair Cook serenely on his way once again.

Then I was bowled by Hilfenhaus. It was an in-swinger from around the wicket. I tried to flick it and it just held up a bit. It was actually a very good ball from an awkward angle. I was disappointed – getting my twentieth Test hundred would have been a great way to finish the series. But I was happy with the way I played because I had wrested the initiative back after their tail had wagged, and Cookie and I had set a good platform for a big score. After that, there were a couple of sucker punches. In the next over, Jonathan Trott was out early for once, then KP made 36 before being caught by Beer on the boundary off Johnson. That was a bad way to finish the day, having been in a great position to nail them down.

We felt slightly disappointed as we headed back to our apartments in Star City. It's a particularly odd thing staying in a casino when you're playing in a cricket match. Star City is a very poor man's Las Vegas. You get all sorts of people from various walks of life, many of whom have just thrown away their life savings and are wandering around in a horrible drunken daze. There are also a lot of rich Chinese who have come over for a holiday. Everything's glitzy and shiny. The suitability of staying at Star City during a Test match in the future would need to be considered.

5 January, Sydney, 5th Test, day 3

End of day 2: Australia 280, England 167–3

I watched us piling on the runs from the seating area in the old pavilion at the SCG. You're right in there with the members. They are very respectful. They don't ask for autographs and photos – they just let you get on with it. But you feel that you have to be careful what you say and do, because you're very much on display. It's one of the great Test match grounds. It's obviously moving on with the times with its new stands, but I love its connection with the history of the game. There are a lot of pictures on the walls of the greats who have played there. As you'd expect, there's a lot of Don Bradman around.

There are also a couple of conventions in the dressing room. One involves a big cupboard which people use as an unofficial honours board. Anyone who gets a hundred in a state or international game writes it up there and signs their name. There's also the odd impromptu comment from team-mates – next to Stuart Law's name someone had written 'Australian cricket legend!!' It's a link with all the games that have been played there in the past. By the end of the day, both Cook and Bell had added their names.

Cook was completely at ease with himself and his game. He just kept batting. A few players have done that against us in the past – Mike Hussey, both in this series and in 2006–07, Chanderpaul for the West Indies, Jayawardene for Sri Lanka – guys in such good nick that it feels almost impossible to get them out. It hasn't happened so much with our own players in the past; they've made hundreds, but not three or four in a row. But now Cook's tally of runs was becoming phenomenal. It was remarkable – his hunger, his desire, the way he recognised that the team needed him to keep playing well.

He was up there with the most runs ever in an Ashes series. We started calling him The Don. We were saying 'Well done, Don,' and joking about it, but everyone in the side was genuinely delighted for the bloke. No one deserved it more. He's very modest and self-effacing about his success. He and I always have a laugh when we're compared to some of the greats in the game. Our opening-partnership total had recently passed that of Hobbs and Sutcliffe – and we were saying, 'Who would have thought it,when all we do is nick it to third man and whack one off our legs past fine leg.'

Cook was very selective in the shots he played. He cut very well. He drove well through extra cover, though he didn't do it often – he just picked the right balls. Batting is simple, as long as you pick the right balls to play the right shots to. If you've been out there a long time and are comfortable with your game, it seems like the easiest thing in the world. You think, 'There's a half-volley – I'll hit it for four. That's a length ball – I'll leave it alone.' When you're out of form, you're wondering, 'Is this a half-volley? Is it drivable? I'll give it a go. Oh no, I've nicked it – I wasn't quite there.' There are so many things going through your mind, you begin to think that no one's ever going to bowl you a half-volley or a drag-down ball again. They're just going to hit that length time and time again and eventually you're going to nick one. It's amazing how your mindset changes. And to a certain extent, opposition teams respond to the fact that you're out of form and bowl better at you.

Ian Bell had never made a hundred against Australia. Throughout the tour, he had been oozing quality, looking like a man at the peak of his powers. He used to have a reputation for not scoring runs when it mattered. He put that to bed with his performance against Australia at The Oval in 2009, and in South Africa after that he played a couple of really good innings under pressure. So the only thing left to prove was getting a hundred against Australia. He'd had the opportunity to do it a few times in the series, but he finally took his chance at Sydney with 115. It was a magnificent innings – there's no one in world cricket who looks better than Ian Bell when he's going, and it will set him up brilliantly for future Ashes series. Meanwhile, it also put us in an impregnable position.

6 January, Sydney, 5th Test, day 4

End of day 3: Australia 280, England 488–7

Paul Collingwood took Andy and me to one side in the morning. He said, 'Look, I just want to let you know that I'm going to retire at the end of the game. I want to tell the lads – is it okay if I tell them now? I want to announce it before the game's over so that I can go out and enjoy my final few days playing for England.' And we agreed that he should tell them. I also said a few words. It was certainly a bit emotional, because he's a good friend of mine and he's given so much to the England team over the years.

When we had a quiet moment I said to him that I thought it was the right time to go, and that in my mind he'd over-achieved as an England cricketer, massively, so it shouldn't be a sad day, it should be a very happy day – and when he's sitting in the dressing room at the end of the game he should be incredibly proud of what he's done with his career. He's an honest bloke, and he said he felt that when he was in good form he was up there with anyone in the world, but his technique didn't allow him to be in good form enough, which was his one frustration. And to carry on playing, he felt he would have to make a lot of changes to his game, which it was too late to do.

We'll only recognise what he did for the team when he's gone, because he does so many little things. There's his presence in the dressing room, what he says in meetings. He's passionate, and the most important thing he brings to the side is that selflessness – the belief that the team is more important than anything, and that he'll do anything for it. That's why he throws himself round on the field; that's why he bowls his overs even when his leg's falling off; that's why he'll stay in when the team needs him to bat all day and only get 40; that's why he'll get caught at long-on when he could have played for himself and been not out. No one demonstrated what we're about as a side more than Paul Collingwood, and that's why he'll be missed so much.

Disappointingly, he had got out for 13 the day before, lofting one to long-on. I thought he'd go out and play aggressively, and he did. And annoyingly, and incredibly frustratingly for him, it wasn't going to be a fairy tale ending, but as he said himself, for players like him, maybe fairy tales don't come true.

Prior really rubbed the Australians' noses in it on the fourth day. The game was in the balance for quite a long time, then Bell and Cook took the game away from them, and finally Prior drove the initiative home. In this game he got one of the fastest ever Ashes hundreds for England, off 109 balls, playing brilliantly against the spinners in particular.

By the time he was out for 118, Australia were staring at another innings defeat. Our final total was 644, which was the best England score since the match against India at Lord's in 1990 when Graham Gooch made his 333. Funnily enough, I was there. That match was my first live experience of Test cricket.

We had them seven down by the end of the day. It was always asking quite a lot for us to bowl them out, even after claiming the extra half-hour. It was worth trying, though, because the Barmy Army were going mental; we'd steamrollered through the Australian top order, and it would have been a fitting end to the series if we could have finished it off that evening.

It didn't work, but once again it was a genuinely outstanding bowling performance. Reverse swing proved Australia's undoing. Anderson, Bresnan, Tremlett – all were incredibly difficult to play. Clarke was completely strokeless against Anderson, almost mesmerised. The wickets went in a blur. (I could have tried Collingwood towards the end of the day when the others were tiring, but he told me not to bowl him in the second innings so that his Hussey wicket could be his last ball in Test cricket!)

Sitting down in the dressing room at the end of that fourth day, we knew we had the Test match won. We could actually enjoy ourselves for once. There was no need to worry about Australia coming back at us. We were utterly dominant; everything was going our way. We already had the Ashes in the bag, and now we could really enjoy the moment. And you could tell – the confidence with which the bowlers bowled was there for everyone to see. We knew that the final day might be a little bit frustrating, but the job was pretty much done.

So we had a beer to celebrate three more hundreds. We'd had a lot of beers to celebrate a lot of hundreds in this series. It was brilliant! Old school – proper old school.

17

LAST RITES

7 January 2011, Sydney, 5th Test, day 5

End of day 4: Australia 280 & 213–7, England 644

THAT last session – taking the final three wickets – was actually quite painful. It was amazing how many members of the Barmy Army were there to celebrate it, and as is always the case, it takes longer than you want. Siddle hung around for quite a long time with Smith, but eventually he whacked one from Swann down deep midwicket's throat, and then we removed the final two pretty quickly. There were incredible scenes all round the ground – the Barmy Army went ballistic. We got on stage to receive the Ashes as a group, and it was an incredibly proud moment for me to get my hands on that replica Ashes urn, even though for some reason they wanted to give us a big trophy instead, which I thought was ridiculous. The presentation ceremony was poor actually, but we didn't care – it was our moment.

I had a feeling of immense pride that we'd finished off the job and beaten Australia by an innings three times in an Ashes series, something that I honestly believe will never be done again. History had been made. What happens in future Ashes series will put this series into context, but I know that those of us involved in it will always see it as one of those rare times in life when all the stars are aligned – everyone was at the peak of their powers and we achieved something as a group of blokes that was very special. And we broke new ground, which doesn't happen very often.

I know English teams have won out here before, but not for a long time, not in our generation, not in the generation before us, and we'd done it in our own way. We didn't have any amazingly quick bowlers or mystery spinners – it was a triumph of persistence and teamwork, planning and execution. And by the end, Australia had no answers.

The celebrations were great. Andy and I both gave speeches to the lads about what we'd achieved and how proud we were, and we sang the team song. Swanny got it going, as usual. Later, I took a call from the prime minister, who congratulated us on winning the Ashes. We'd had probably three hours of drinking beer by then, so I was a bit paranoid about what I was going to say to him. I think I just about got away with it, and he was obviously genuinely delighted for us.

We finally had a beer with the Aussies. That was good. We had refrained from doing so throughout the series for sound reasons, but when the series is over it's good to let your guard down and discuss all the incidents from the matches. The Aussies are always fun to talk to and good lads. I spoke with Ricky Ponting, Michael Clarke, Phil Hughes. I also had quite a long chat with Justin Langer, the Australian batting coach.

You don't exactly have an air of superiority as you walk in

there, but it can be awkward for the team that's been beaten badly. You don't really know what to say or do. You can say, 'Well played,' but at the back of your mind, you might be thinking, 'You've had an absolute shocker.' In cricket, you understand that you're going to win some and lose some, and therefore even when you're a winner, you appreciate what the losers have been through. And you also know that the Ashes in particular is a celebration of all that's good in cricket. Both of the teams appreciated that they were very lucky and honoured to have represented their country in that series.

Later on, the families came into the dressing room, and my sons Sam and Luca were holding the little Ashes urn and fighting over whose Ashes it was – Sam's or Luca's. Then we went out and played some cricket on the square. What we'd achieved was amazing, and it was even better that my family were there to celebrate it with me.

The best part of that whole day came at about five o'clock. The supporters and the media had gone home and the families had left. The players and support staff all went out into the middle of the SCG square. There were probably twenty of us sitting in a circle having a beer when David Saker started talking about what he remembered about the series and how proud he was. Eoin Morgan said a few words, and then, without prompting, we went round the whole circle, and everyone spoke about their memories of the tour – on and off the field.

It was like sitting round a campfire. There we were, in the middle of the ground, reminiscing about what we'd been through, and the hairs on the back of my neck were standing up. It probably went on for an hour. Up to that point, we'd always had the next game to worry about, but suddenly it was hitting us – what we'd been through, why we'd done so well and why we'll always remember it as the highlight of our careers.

I was in a light-hearted mood by then – I'd done my serious bit earlier. In South Africa we had come up with the idea of a thought for the day; at any stage someone could be called on to give one, and there were various different quotes and proverbs. When it was my turn I'd recounted most of the 'Wear Sunscreen' song produced by Baz Luhrmann. It starts off: 'Wear sunscreen. If I could offer you one tip for the future, sunscreen would be it. The long-term benefits of sunscreen have been proved by scientists, whereas the rest of my advice has no basis more reliable than my own meandering experience. I will dispense this advice now.' Then it goes on: 'Enjoy the power and beauty of your youth . . . Oh, never mind – you will not understand the power and beauty of your youth until they're faded.' And it continues in that vein.

It actually started life as a column in a paper written by Mary Schmich, but there are some amazing little snippets in it. It went down quite well in South Africa because I'd spent a lot of time learning it. Ever since then it'd been something of a running joke. So in that circle in Sydney I simply said, 'Lads, I'm just incredibly proud of how we managed to continue wearing sunscreen throughout the whole tour . . .' There were laughs all round. It was a bit of an in-joke.

I didn't say so at the time, but if I had to pick an abiding memory of the tour it would actually be a moment from the Perth Test. It was Ponting getting out to Anderson, caught by Collingwood with that diving catch. The reason is that we had taken down their captain – their most experienced player – by putting the ball exactly where we wanted to, and backing that up with outstanding fielding. That was the series in a nutshell: taking on people who are used to playing on those wickets, and have amazing records there, and backing ourselves to beat them by doing the basics very well and doing it as a team. I know that if we'd seen the opposition dismissing our captain in that manner, we'd have been saying to ourselves, 'We've gone here – we can't compete with these guys.'

Eventually, we went back to the hotel and then out to the Flying Fish to celebrate. Everyone: wives and kids were there as well. There were well-wishers everywhere. In fact, the Barmy Army seemed to have taken over the whole city! It was a great night. But by eleven o'clock I was in no state to be doing anything and had to be escorted to bed by my wife. It had been a long day, a long match and a long series, and finally, the healthy mix of alcohol, exhilaration and exhaustion caught up with me. Some of the other lads seemed to have rather more stamina.

18

WHERE DID IT ALL GO RIGHT?

W E went straight into the one-day series after the Tests, so we didn't have a lot of time to think about what we had achieved. But later, on our very last day in Australia, we were in Perth and the former Australian fast bowler Ashley Noffke offered to take six or seven of us out on his boat up to Rottnest Island and to a couple of the isolated beaches there.

We were sitting at the front of the boat crashing over the waves. The one-day series was over, and we were all just looking back on what we'd achieved over the last three months. It was our first opportunity to get out of the bubble since the Ashes – away from the hotel/practice/play routine. It was great to be out in the fresh air that day, and it's quite wild there. When you're on the water and the waves are crashing around you, it's a bit like staring into a fire – you can't help getting reflective. It was amazing how quiet everyone was, and for me it was the first time I was really able to let go and indulge myself.

I will always remember how motivated that group of guys were – not just when we arrived in Australia, but months before that. Everyone was absolutely committed to making sure we seized our opportunity, and the whole experience brought us very close together as a group. The good days, the bad days, the travelling, being surrounded by media, by supporters – whenever we meet up in years to come, we'll have that special bond there. The memory of going through something extraordinary can never be taken away from us, and whatever we go on to achieve from here, anyone who loves the game of cricket in our country will always look back on this series with satisfaction that the ambition of winning in Australia had been achieved. It may well happen again, but I doubt it will be in the same manner.

I was with Matt Prior, Ian Bell and Jonathan Trott; Broady and Anderson were there as well. What amazed me was that though we hadn't performed well in the one-day series – in fact, we'd been beaten comprehensively – the sense of achievement still hadn't dimmed. There was an overwhelming feeling of pride in having represented England and brought so much joy to so many people, including ourselves; pride in each other's performances and in the hard work, in pushing ourselves as far as our bodies would take us, not just on the pitch, but in Germany and in fitness sessions. And then there was the thorough enjoyment of it. We're always striving to improve and thinking about the next thing, but you also have to enjoy the ride along the way, and I really felt that the guys switched on to that very early. Of course, you enjoy a tour a lot more when you're winning, but the attitude and the spirit everyone showed were fantastic from the start.

Left The 6ft 8in Chris Tremlett stood tall in more ways than one when he replaced the injured Stuart Broad in Perth, bowling Philip Hughes with his sixth ball and taking eight wickets in the match.

Below left Mitchell Johnson was dropped for the Second Test but returned in Perth to bludgeon 62, Australia's top first-innings score, after we had reduced them to 69 for 5 on the first day.

Below right Perth was Mitchell Johnson's match. Their first-innings total of 268 looked modest, only for the Queenslander to rip through our top order and help Australia to level the series.

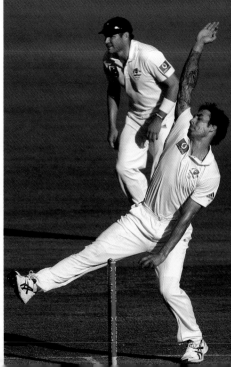

Tim Bresnan made a belated but decisive appearance in the series, sparking scenes of wild rejoicing by dislodging Ben Hilfenhaus in Melbourne to ensure we kept the Ashes.

A pat on the head for Chris Tremlett after Kevin Pietersen's catch removes opener Shane Watson on the first morning in Melbourne, the first blow for Australia as they are all out for 98.

Tremlett collects another of his four first-innings wickets, Ricky Ponting's torment with the bat continuing as the ball heads for the hands of Graeme Swann with his score on 10.

other ton for Jonathan Trott, whose 168 not t in Melbourne contributed to a first-nings lead of 415 which allowed us to press me our advantage over the Aussies.

The heat of moment sees Ricky Ponting remonstrate with umpire Aleem Dar after an unsuccessful review of a not-out decision in Kevin Pietersen's favour on day two at the MCG.

retain the Ashes with a match to spare by winning the Fourth Test in Melbourne and the ervescent Graeme Swann leads the 'sprinkler dance' before the Barmy Army.

Left Alastair Cook on course for a total of 189 in the Fifth Test in Sydney, taking his series aggregate to a magnificent 766 runs and sapping Australian morale as surely as it boosted ours.

Below The final innings of the series brought me 60 runs off balls before I was bowled. Hundreds for Alastair Cook, Bell and Matt Prior put us on course for a third innings victory.

right Michael Beer's Test debut after a handful of first-class games intensified the criticism in Australia, complaints which the young spinner's figures of 1 for 112 scarcely assuaged.

below Matt Prior hits out in his quickfire 118 in the Fifth Test, a typically feisty way to finish a series which for him began with a golden duck as the second victim in Peter Siddle's hat-trick.

After 11 fifties in four Ashes series, Ian Bell's persistence and sheer quality produce the century he craved against Australia to put us in an impregnable position in Sydney.

Chris Tremlett forces Michael Beer to chop the ball on to his stumps. Our 3–1 series success is complete, the cue for beer of a different kind and a drink with the Australians.

e celebrations in Sydney, marking a triumph of persistence, teamwork, planning and
·cution by a side without any frighteningly fast bowlers or unfathomable spinners.

red elation at the SCG with vice-captain Alastair Cook, whose astounding batting feats
ned the nickname of The Don, as in Bradman, and the man of the series award.

This one went for six in my 1[5?] against India in our tied group match during the 2011 World Cup, but we also lost to Ireland and Bangladesh while the Indians went on to win the trophy in style.

My wife Ruth and children Sa[m] and Luca (*in my arms*) welcom[e] me back to England after five months of uncompromising, almost relentless cricket in far[-] flung places.

Looking back at the Ashes, I think the fundamental reasons we won were that when our batsmen got in, they went on to get big scores, while our bowlers were able to master the Australian conditions and produce conventional swing, reverse swing and accuracy.

Pushing on to make big scores was something we had talked about on numerous occasions, but it was one of the first times that all our batsmen managed to achieve it. With the bat, we got through the first fifteen overs more times than not. Once you're through that period, the batsmen themselves are as likely to have a role in their own downfall as the bowlers – especially without Shane Warne playing. In the past we'd succumbed to frustration or lack of patience; this time we didn't do that. The best examples were Alastair Cook and Jonathan Trott.

One of the reasons was that Cook went back to his old technique. He'd had a tough summer. People had told him his technique didn't work and he'd have to change it, so he did change it. I was always a little bit suspicious of his new technique, because I thought it eradicated some of his strengths without necessarily covering his weaknesses, but when the going got tough for him, he sensibly went back to what he knew. It started with a hundred against Pakistan at The Oval, and then he stuck with it in Australia, trusting that what he'd done over the last six or seven years would hold him in good stead when the pressure was at its greatest. Cricket is not a complicated game, but we tend to make it a lot more complicated than we should. Alastair went back to keeping it simple, and it paid dividends for him.

What the bowlers all did very well was to realise that on any given day their role was likely to change. At times Graeme Swann was a defensive bowler; at times he was our attacking threat. Sometimes the ball was swinging, in which case the likes of Jimmy Anderson were a handful; at other times it wasn't swinging, and we had to hang in there and make sure we did everything we could to get the ball reversing. Reacting well to the changing circumstances of a game was a real strength for us.

Alongside that, our fielding was a big part of our success. Hanging on to every chance we got, just about, creating pressure, getting run-outs – it all helped to cultivate a feeling within the Australian team that they were under siege and that they weren't going to be let off the hook.

Our running between the wickets was also very good. If you look at how many run-outs we had and how many run-outs Australia had, you might think that it was because they were pushing our fielders harder and taking more risks, but I thought we got it about right. We put their fielders under pressure, but we did it smartly.

Ultimately, the ruthlessness we showed is not something that's been synonymous with English cricket generally. Perhaps it's a sign of the England team graduating to the next level. All the best sides have had it in the past – and we had displayed it against the side traditionally associated with ruthlessness more than any other. You get that ruthlessness by having a longer-term goal, and pushing yourself beyond just one series. You get it by not relying on one or two players, because if you do that, eventually they're not going to perform and you'll come crashing down to earth.

We achieved all that through team unity and people being unselfish – not seeking the limelight but working for each other. One of the real pluses of the tour was that everyone understood what this series meant; they understood what lay at the end of it if we played well, and so they resolved to give everything they had in order to achieve it. That wasn't just three or four players – that was every member of the squad.

Andy Flower is of course a massive figure, who has played a huge part in England's resurgence over the last couple of years. He has galvanised the management team. He's brought in some new people and really upped the levels of professionalism and organisation. The way they prepare us during practices is a major step on from previous regimes.

He once went to an American football training session and noticed how structured and organised every training session was. The coaches were there for at least an hour before the players arrived, organising what they were likely to do. He's brought that into the cricket environment, so now the coaches plan a practice session well beforehand; they get there early and set up all the various drills. When the players arrive everything is structured to make the best use of the time available. That's a big change. In cricket generally, we can be too content to do what we've always done – both as players and as coaches.

The relationship between captain and coach is absolutely crucial, and I can't speak highly enough of how Andy takes the pressure off me personally. He's incredibly respectful of my position as captain, but also as a batsman, and he tries to take as much pressure off my shoulders as he can, without diminishing my role as a captain and as a leader. He does a lot of the important stuff I haven't got enough time for – some of the talking to players, some of the organising, some of the liaising with the ECB.

He allows me to get on with the job of captaining on the field and preparing myself for my own game, as well as managing the players individually and communicating with them. He exudes old-fashioned honesty and respect. Everyone knows where they stand with him – he's not someone who'll talk about people behind their backs. He's completely honest with them about how he feels they're playing. He respects their position; he's never fallen into the trap of saying, 'Test cricket's easy. I should know – I've done it. So why can't you play a certain shot; why can't you play a certain way?'

He understands the difficulties, the mental challenges, the mental hurdles, but at the same time he doesn't like excuses and he doesn't like people who aren't willing to commit themselves fully to what they're doing. Over the years I've been involved in the England team, there have always been a few people in the side discontented with the management or the captain or other players. Since Andy's been at the helm we've had very few instances of that, if any.

On the batting side, he will suggest things to me occasionally, but mainly he lets me use him as a sounding board. I probably consult him more than any of the other coaches. So if I'm struggling with my play against spin or against a certain bowler, I'll talk it through with him. And obviously I have great respect for his opinions on batting as a left-hander. I suppose I'm a bit long in the tooth to be radically altering my game, but I think Andy understands my game pretty well now, and therefore will give me advice that's suitable for me rather than what the textbook might recommend.

Bouncing through the waves on that boat, I thought that never has an England team been in a better place to go on and achieve the goal of becoming the best side in the world. Over three months in Australia we'd proved to ourselves and to others that we could perform in different conditions, that we could cope with real pressure and expectation, that we could stick together when the going got tough – the best sides always have these attributes. To become the number one side in the world, you need to win at home and away consistently. Consistency is probably the biggest challenge for us, but with a relatively young group of players who should only get better, we have every reason to believe that we can carry on improving. If we do that enough over the coming months and years, then that goal of being the number one team in the world doesn't seem so far away.

We had a lovely day swimming, snorkelling and larking about on Rottnest. It was our last day in Australia and it was very therapeutic. It finished in a slightly less celebratory manner, however. We had had to leave the keys to our bus with the boatyard owner, who promptly went home with them. So when we arrived back from the island, we were in a panic about getting to the airport in time. Thankfully, we managed to summon a couple of cabs and just made it onto the flight home.

19

WORLD CUP WOES

1 April 2011

I'VE been back for five days now. It's strange having two almost completely separate lives. I'm at home at the moment, playing with the kids, doing the school run, feeding the sheep, whereas a week ago we were in Colombo preparing for the World Cup quarter-final. Arriving back after that defeat, I felt emotionally and physically shot to pieces.

It's been a bit like running a marathon. You have enough energy to make it to the finishing line but once you've passed it, there's nothing left in the tank. That's how I feel. A complete veil of fatigue engulfed me once I got that final press conference out of the way after the Sri Lanka game. In the week or two leading up to that match, the hardest thing was continuing to make clear, well-thought-out decisions.

I don't think I'm alone in feeling this. One look at the bedraggled bunch that hopped onto the plane with me showed that every one of us had given all they could over the course of a very long and arduous winter. It was now time to go home to families, rest up, regroup and get ready for the next challenges. Here's what had happened.

9 February, Marlow

I'm staring at my suitcase; it hasn't been unpacked from Australia but I'm putting last-minute provisions in to tide me over for six weeks in the subcontinent. Not necessarily food, but DVDs and some cheap and nasty clothes rather than the swish ones. Not that I've got too many of the latter. I've got *The Pacific* to watch, which should provide a good ten or twelve hours' worth of entertainment on lonely nights in Dhaka or Chittagong. I made sure I got some *Top Gear* downloaded as well.

More than anything, I'm just trying to get my head around the fact that I'm leaving again. I'm finding it hard to broach the subject that I'm going again to my kids. They're just getting used to Dad being at home again. Ruth's going to fly out for a few days in the middle of the World Cup, but I'm not going to see the kids for six weeks or so. It's going to be hard to say goodbye again at the airport.

I have to change my kit completely. There's a special England kit for the World Cup, so all the old Australian stuff goes into plastic bags to be auctioned off or sent to charities. And with three kit bags and my golf clubs, here we go again.

16 February, Dhaka, Bangladesh

There was a lot of talk about us being fatigued heading into the tournament, but one of the things I found on arrival was that it was quite a vibrant, energising atmosphere. All the other teams in the world were there, and there was a great sense of anticipation and excitement about what was to come. There were enormous cricket bats and pictures of Tamim Iqbal plastered all over billboards. Bangladesh had spent a lot of time and effort and money preparing itself for the tournament.

We arrived with a lot of preparation still to do. Even though we'd played seven one-dayers in Australia, we had to get used to very different conditions, very quickly. Australia and Bangladesh must be the two countries in the world least like each other in terms of cricketing conditions – Australia, generally good bounce and carry; Bangladesh, slow and low. So the shots that we'd been relying on in Australia, pulls and cuts, had to be put in the locker and replaced with sweeps and dabs.

From a team point of view, we also had to work out our best side for those conditions very quickly. We were fortunate that Stuart Broad was fully fit and that Tim Bresnan and Ajmal Shahzad were coming back to fitness. We were hopeful that within four or five days of arriving we would have a full squad to pick from for the first time since the end of the Ashes.

The first big decision was to promote Kevin Pietersen to the top of the order. There were two reasons. First, we recognised that taking advantage of the first ten or fifteen overs in the subcontinent was going to be very important. Someone who could play big shots, strong shots down the ground, and also go over the top if necessary, was vitally important. But we also wanted someone who could then go on and play a substantial innings. It was a bit of a radical departure from what we'd done in the past and it was hardly ideal that KP was doing it for the first time in a practice match a week before the World Cup started, but for KP, the combination of having the chance to bat through the innings and doing it in the World Cup was something that floated his boat.

We had a couple of practice matches. We played some pretty shoddy cricket against Canada, but then we really raised our game against Pakistan and beat them very comfortably. It was the beginning of a bit of a trend – against the lesser nations we almost dropped down to their level, and against the better sides we upped our level to match or exceed them.

22 February, Nagpur, India, Group B: v Netherlands

I don't think anyone would call Nagpur one of the must-see venues in India, although the ground was new and impressive. Holland's Ryan ten Doeschate is one of a new generation of what you might call cricket mercenaries. He has a very special set of skills which are particularly suited to Twenty20 cricket and he's making the most of his career, travelling around the world, playing for as many sides as he can in as many Twenty20 competitions as possible. He's a clever bowler. But his strength is in his batting. He has a good mix – he has a smart cricket brain and can manoeuvre singles pretty well, but he's also able to play some big shots when the situation requires.

In their innings, we got a little stuck in the batting power-play, in particular when they played all sorts of cricket/hockey shots. It was the first time our bowlers recognised that what had worked for us in the past – the slow-ball bouncers and short balls – wasn't necessarily going to work so well over here. We dropped a lot of catches, and we all sensed we should be doing a lot better, but on a flat wicket we were finding it hard to make things happen and ten Doeschate made the most of the let-off we gave him to score an excellent one-day hundred.

One of the things I was very conscious to do in the break, having conceded 292 runs, was to allow the emotion to die down in the dressing room for ten or fifteen minutes. I let the guys calm down and then I made it very clear to them that 290 was actually the par score on that ground and that if we played smart cricket, we'd chase them down relatively easily. Thankfully that was what transpired – after a couple of hiccups.

27 February, Bangalore, India, Group B: v India

The contrast between the sparse surroundings at Nagpur and the incredibly plush new flat-screen TVs and massage chairs at the M Chinnaswamy Stadium was a pleasant surprise and one that made our stay feel more homely. Before the India match, which we'd earmarked as one of the crucial games of the tournament, we played some golf on some of the most unbelievably manicured fairways I've ever seen. One day I saw some women plucking loads of grass off the fairways. Golf had a significance because when you're batting in those low, slow subcontinental conditions, you have to be prepared to put pace on the ball. And the best way I've found to do that is to employ a variation on my golf swing. I try to give myself a bit of room, free my arms and hit it on a similar plane to a golf shot.

I arrived at the ground in Bangalore with an incredible feeling – real excitement mixed with butterflies. The crowds were already there and you could feel the buzz, and because we were playing India, the favourites to win the World Cup, it was almost as if there was nothing to lose. I sensed it was going to be a special occasion and it was.

Sachin Tendulkar played remarkably well, although he slightly surprised us by not going out particularly hard. He batted quite slowly in the beginning – with Tendulkar, you never feel as if he's bludgeoning you away. Then he took on our bowlers in the middle overs and gave India impetus at a time when our game plan was to restrict the scoring. Fortunately, the batting powerplay gave us a way in. Sachin got out and in the last six or seven overs, India lost their way and ended up getting 'only' 338.

We had the run chase well in hand until I received a great yorker from Zaheer Khan to end my innings. I was forced to watch the final overs nervously as we swayed from having the game in the bag to having no chance, before eventually salvaging a tie. My 158 was without doubt my finest one-day innings. First, it was my highest score in one-day cricket. Second, it was against India, the favourites, on their own patch, in a World Cup – you don't get a much bigger stage than that. Having conceded 338, as captain I really needed to lead the response and to show enough fitness to cope with batting for a long period after a long, hot afternoon in the field. So it was an innings I was really proud of, right up there with any of the Ashes hundreds I've scored, because I manipulated the field so well.

I thought we were two decent overs away from winning it when we took the powerplay. But Bell went down with cramp and the momentum was lost. We should have won easily, but before the game we probably would've taken a tie and, as Dhoni said to me during the post-match presentation, a tie was as good as a win in terms of qualification, because it was one point you had that an opposition team didn't have.

2 March, Bangalore, India, Group B: v Ireland

This would have to go down as my worst birthday ever. It's one of our routines that if it's someone's birthday, the team masseur Mark Saxby is in charge of getting a card signed by the players and before the start we all get in a huddle and the card's handed over. In this case Mark actually forgot that it was my birthday, and when Mark Nicholas mentioned it at the toss, it sent Saxby scurrying around in a blind panic trying to sort something out.

Of course, I was hoping for a reasonably comfortable day on the cricket pitch followed by a couple of beers in the evening and perhaps a bit of reminiscing about what had happened over the previous twelve months. That happy dream was shattered with every blow from Kevin O'Brien's bat. We had them at 111 for 5 chasing 327, and things were going nice and smoothly, when O'Brien came in and chanced his arm, and before we knew it he had 100 off 50 balls. It was one of the greatest examples of clean hitting that I've seen. By the end we didn't know where to bowl to him.

So my post-match birthday drink was a very sombre and chastening experience, especially when I heard 'Happy Birthday Dear Straussy' wafting down the hallway of our hotel from the Irish celebrations. I could appreciate what a great day it had been for Irish cricket, but I wish it had been at someone else's expense!

11 March, Chittagong, Bangladesh, Group B: v Bangladesh
Kevin Pietersen going home was a big loss for us. He was just starting to get used to the role of opening the batting. He and I had proved quite good foils for each other at the top of the order. But he went into the South Africa game really struggling with his hernia. He was obviously on some quite strong medication to limit the pain, but at the end of the game he felt it was impossible for him to carry on.

We were pretty excited about the thought of Eoin Morgan coming back in. If you're going to lose KP, you want him to be replaced by someone who's pretty damn good. When we had left for the World Cup, our information was that Morgan wasn't going to be available, but subsequently he was told he didn't need an operation on his finger. He made an immediate impact against Bangladesh with a superb fifty. Having not played for five or six weeks, it was an astounding effort.

Potentially the bigger blow was Stuart Broad going home early for the second time in the winter with another side strain, which he had incurred during an outstanding spell of bowling to take us to a very surprising and unexpected victory against South Africa five days before. He'd shown in the games he did play in the World Cup that he was our leading wicket-taking option in those conditions, and he was certainly going to be very tough to replace. None of our other bowlers had his combination of pace, bounce and nous.

The defeat against Bangladesh was even more disappointing than the Ireland game. We didn't bat particularly well, but again we had them at 169 for 8 and just needed to take the final two wickets against guys whose batting records were very poor, and we weren't able to do it. We were all enormously frustrated at the end of that game.

Jimmy Anderson in particular looked as if he'd given all he could to the side. He'd had incredible demands placed on him throughout the course of the winter. He was the one player who'd managed to avoid injury, but he was now getting a few niggles, and when you combine that with a very tired and worn-out mind, by the end of the World Cup he just wasn't able to do what he wanted to do.

17 March, Chennai, India, Group B: v West Indies

This was a must-win game, and though we had been away from home for five months, none of us wanted to leave in those circumstances. We'd played some very inconsistent cricket in the World Cup up to that point, but after everything else we'd done over the winter we certainly didn't want to bow out of the competition in the group stages. So there was a lot of motivation.

I had to tell Jimmy Anderson he wasn't playing. It was a hard conversation for me to have. It was sad that a guy who'd been so instrumental in all our achievements had to be left out because he was just not physically capable of continuing. He'd given everything, and he should be applauded for carrying on and for never once complaining.

We decided to throw caution to the wind in our selection. We left out Collingwood and Anderson, and Shahzad was injured, so we replaced them with James Tredwell, Chris Tremlett and Luke Wright. Three World Cup debutants, but fresh blood. They repaid us handsomely with some very fine performances. Firstly Wright scored a very valuable 44 at the end of the innings when we were teetering on the edge. And then Tredwell struck to get Chris Gayle out – a massive wicket after he'd smacked our bowlers everywhere on his way to 43.

Tredwell went on to take three more incredibly valuable wickets at a time when West Indies looked as if they were going to cruise to victory.

Then Jonathan Trott caught Andre Russell on the boundary, and may or may not have just touched the rope as he caught it. The moment it was given as six runs, we all could've been forgiven for thinking, 'This isn't meant to be.' But we remained calm, and the feeling on the field was that this will happen, just keep believing. And in the end it did.

It was an easy game to captain. We had to keep looking for wickets at all times, so you had to have men round the bat, mix up the bowling and keep asking questions of them – and thankfully a lot of those questions remained unanswered. It was a great victory, and the passion in the huddle at the end of the game showed that the spirit of the England side remained strong. We headed to the quarter-final feeling that we could still upset a couple of the big boys.

26 March, Colombo, Sri Lanka, quarter-final: v Sri Lanka
The build-up to the World Cup quarter-final was not ideal. For starters, we had eight days off. At that stage of the tournament, having been away for so long and having played so much cricket, we wanted to keep going instead of sitting around in hotel rooms.

I think it was that as much as anything that took Mike Yardy over the edge. He had been battling with depression for quite a long time, reaching back into the summer in England.

He was working with a doctor, his own specialist, and I gained an understanding that it was getting harder for him, but I thought it was likely that he would be able to see it through to the end of the World Cup.

In the end, he reached a stage where he just had to say he couldn't carry on. He wasn't able to sleep, he wasn't able to give any consideration to his cricket, so he went to Andy Flower and said, 'Look, I'm no good to you; I have to go home.' Which in a lot of ways is a courageous decision, but in the end it was the only decision he could take. There was no other option for him.

Some people are affected by depression and for those people international cricket is always going to be tough. It was tough for Marcus Trescothick; he battled it for a long time before he just couldn't do it any more. The great stress, the lack of a family network, the endless hours on your own and all the travelling can be fairly dispiriting at the best of times. All of those things combined can make it very difficult if you have those tendencies. Most people muddle through one way or another, because most people don't actually suffer from depression; they just have bad days.

The statistics said that the team batting first in Colombo tended to win. Thankfully, we won the toss. But things didn't really go to plan after that. I struggled against Dilshan. It was the first time in the World Cup I had faced off-spin right from the start, and on that wicket there was no angle to work with. It wasn't turning but it was keeping very low. So in the first ten overs the majority of the fielders were up in the ring, and to score, you had to go down the wicket and whack them over his head. I had one of those days when everything I tried didn't come off.

Jonathan Trott and Ravi Bopara rebuilt well and got us into a position where if we had had a really good last ten overs we could have got to 260-odd, but we probably won't be the last side to suffer at the hands of their bowling attack at the end of the innings. Malinga was very hard to get away in the powerplays, Murali used every ounce of his experience, and against Mendis bowling very straight, you had to take some pretty big risks to get him away.

Our score was well below par and from that moment on we were relying on getting a couple of early wickets and building enough pressure to force more, because we knew the pitch itself was playing very well. Unfortunately, it wasn't meant to be. Tharanga and Dilshan both played exceptionally well, our bowlers weren't able to find a way in, and no matter how much we chopped and changed and tried different things, they were able to answer all the questions. We lost heavily by ten wickets and it was what we deserved.

We lost to a better side, a more balanced side for those conditions, and we left the World Cup knowing that our chance of winning had gone and that we weren't good enough. It brought home just how far we need to improve to compete with those guys in those conditions in the future. It was a humbling experience. It wasn't the way we would have liked our winter to end but we had reached the end of the road. We came up against a better side, and spirit and togetherness can only take you so far. You need to have quality there, and by that stage of the tournament, for whatever reason, we didn't have enough quality to win.

30 March, going home

Looking back on the whole World Cup campaign, it's clear we made some mistakes. It didn't help that we had to pick the World Cup squad after just one game in the Australia one-day series, when we couldn't know who was going to be in or out of form by the time the World Cup started. That meant that some of our decisions had to be made in hope rather than expectation.

We weren't able to put in the detailed preparation that we were able to put in for the Ashes. In addition, the scheduling did not allow us to play our best cricket in the World Cup – the break the ECB originally scheduled as three weeks had to be reduced when the World Cup was brought forward by countries and players wishing to accommodate the start of the IPL. A lot of people will say that other sides had the same schedule, that Australia had the same schedule. But there is a big difference between playing at home for three months before going to a World Cup, and staying in a hotel for three months before going to a World Cup, especially having asked so much of our players.

By the end, the guys were still giving as much as they could, but there wasn't a huge amount left. But to look at anything other than the quality of our cricket would be to miss the point. English sides have generally struggled in the subcontinent because the conditions don't suit us. The very nature of the pitches means that the local sides have to have bowlers with a lot of variety and they have to have batsmen who play big shots – so that comes very naturally to them.

If I was planning a World Cup campaign now I would spend two or three weeks in somewhere like Dubai, doing a lot of scenario sessions, and middle practices with a completely fresh bunch of players. We left too much to chance. When you are relying on luck or people pulling out performances at the right time, you are going to be let down at some point, and that is what happened with us.

Leaving the World Cup in the quarter-finals takes some gloss off what happened earlier in the winter. But in the full-ness of time, the Ashes will be remembered far more than the World Cup. Maybe that is because of our fascination with history and Australia in general, and the fact that one-day cricket always plays second fiddle to Test cricket for English teams. I don't know if that is healthy, but that is why the Ashes victory will be looked on as a great achievement regardless of what went on afterwards.

There was a bit of a media scrum when we got back. Not of the positive sort, really. There's been a lot of speculation as to what I'm going to do in the future. The World Cup tends to be a kind of watershed, and in that sense, I can understand why it's a talking point. I'm thirty-four years old; it's unlikely I'll play in the next World Cup. That explains my decision to stand down from the one-day captaincy and allow Alastair

Cook to take the team forwards from here. It was a very difficult decision to make, but I felt it was best for the long-term future of England's one-day team.

The nature of sport is that you don't win all the time, and one thing I am very proud of is that the guys stuck together through a long, hard, arduous winter, one in which our resolve and strength and resilience were tested to the full. Maybe that is as important as anything, because it gives you a great springboard to go on and keep improving. We would like to win every game we play, but it is not realistic. All we can do is improve to the extent that we start winning a lot more than we lose.

So to the summer. The number one side in the world, India, now the World Cup champions, are coming to our shores, and so are the runners-up, Sri Lanka. This time we will have the advantage of our own home conditions. At the end of it we will either have taken another significant step forward or we will have drifted back into the pack, both in one-day and Test cricket. Those are the challenges that await us. Those are the challenges that excite us.

Now I'm off to feed those sheep.

20

GOING UP A LEVEL

22 May 2011, Cardiff Castle

A T the start of the summer Andy Flower and I were very conscious that we had to move on from the Ashes. It was easy enough to get motivated for an India series later in the summer, when we would be playing against the number one side in the world; it was less so for an early-season series against Sri Lanka, a few of whose players weren't turning up until the eve of the first Test match, which was likely to be played in cool and blustery conditions.

We had a meeting with the support staff in Loughborough, including Mark Bawden, the psychologist, about how to take things forward. We settled on the catchphrase 'taking things to a new level'. We decided that we weren't going to focus on Sri Lanka or on India; we were going to focus on ourselves and how we could improve on the standards we'd reached in Australia. We had to review our whole set-up. We would get each player to sit down with his specialist coach and map out an individual development plan for the next six months. We looked at our approach to strength and conditioning and how we could improve our fielding. We were determined to use the start of the new summer as a fresh beginning to push on from what we'd achieved.

We felt that it was fitting to hold the first team meeting – the first day back at school, as it were – in something that wasn't just another sterile boardroom in some hotel, and so we managed to get a ballroom in Cardiff Castle. We had a drink and a relaxed meal and a bit of a chat. Andy and I explained how we were looking to take things forward. We also had a lot of statistical information that not only showed how we'd improved over the last eighteen months or so, but also highlighted the areas in which we still weren't world-class. And so I challenged the blokes to address those, and we had a number of small meetings to work out what that would mean in practice.

We split it into categories such as on-field matters, preparation, media and dealing with off-field distractions. There was a lot of positive reinforcement of what we'd done over the last year, but we also drew attention to areas where there was a risk of falling into bad habits.

One of the things the statistics revealed was that over the last eighteen months our bowling had been genuinely world-class, individually and collectively; in fact, we had probably been the best bowling group in the world. But while two or three of our batsmen had pushed on to world's-best level, three or four of the players were still a little short of that. So here we could say that, yes, we have done well, but actually this aspect of our play needs to improve. Over the course of the summer, what was pleasing was how many batsmen got in and made big scores, so that if you looked at our stats at the end of the summer pretty much everyone was up at that level.

Personally, I was aware that I used be very good at going from 50 to 100, but that recently I'd been far less successful. I felt that over the last twelve months I'd perhaps tried to go up through the gears and play a bit more positively, and that had been the cause of my downfall. So it was a question of staying constant throughout the innings – not slow-paced but one-paced. Another area I wanted to address was the number of times I'd been not out overnight, only to get out very quickly the next morning. To remedy this, I had to make sure that my routines in the morning were giving me the best chance of going on and getting runs.

26–30 May 2011, Cardiff, 1st Test v Sri Lanka

It was a game that was blighted by rain. On the fifth day, we were still batting in our first innings, so the chances of a result appeared reasonably slim, particularly as further showers were forecast for that afternoon. That's why I felt, given the balance of probabilities, that an extra few balls to allow Ian Bell to get his hundred before declaring were worth it. If we were going to be in a position to win the game in the afternoon, then it was likely that we'd either get the job done or we wouldn't, and an extra over or two batting wasn't going to make a huge difference either way. So that was the decision I took.

Ian Bell thoroughly deserved that hundred; he played

brilliantly. It was his first of the summer and he ended up getting three more; but you never know, maybe if he hadn't got that one he might not have done so well. You just don't know how things would have turned out, because it also gave us a nice little boost when we went out to bowl – and ultimately we won the game with an inspired performance with the ball on that final afternoon, bowling them out for just 82 runs.

Without Anderson, who was off injured, Tremlett was outstanding at the top. Swann did a brilliant job in the middle, and the momentum we built was very hard for batsmen to resist; you could almost see the panic in their eyes. It was a truly remarkable Test match win. And the great thing for me was that it reconnected us straight away with what we'd done in the winter – great performances, suffocating the opposition – and it put us in a position to build on it.

Unfortunately, the remaining two games in the series were ruined by rain, which prevented us from ramming home winning positions. But it was still a good series win against a decent side, and it allowed us to head towards the India series in good heart, confident that our method was still working well.

It was a very frustrating series for me personally, even though I came into the series in good form, having scored a couple of hundreds for Middlesex. I probably fell into a trap that far too many batsmen fall into. When you get out a couple of times to a certain type of bowling – in my case the left-arm-over of Welagedara – it's easy to feel that you have to change everything you do against them, even though it's worked fine for you in the past. I had made 150 against him earlier in the season and 100 against Glamorgan, who had a left-arm seamer, yet after a couple of failures I was suddenly trying to change my technique. As an experienced player, I was wrong to fall into that trap. I tried to tinker with my set-up – I was getting my 'triggers' out of the way early. But the problem is that the next time you face that bowler you tend to think about your technique rather than the ball. And so I got out. My dismissal in the third Test at the Rose Bowl was a great example of getting caught up in technique rather than simply watching the ball.

So after the series I had some time off – and then went and played against India for Somerset! The idea had been mooted by Andy Flower before the Sri Lanka Test match at Lord's – we were looking ahead to my preparation for the India series. Middlesex didn't have any four-day cricket, so I was thinking of playing a one-dayer or two for them and maybe a couple of second-team games. He said, 'Somerset are playing India; I wonder if we can get you a game there.' My initial reaction was that although I liked the idea of facing the touring side– I think it's always a good thing if you can do that before the series starts – I was very concerned that it had to be something that Somerset also wanted to happen. So a couple of exploratory calls were made. I spoke to Marcus Trescothick and from the word go Somerset were right behind it. They saw it as a way of building some real interest in the game and felt it would be a good thing for their youngsters to have the England captain spend a few days with them. (I think Marcus also saw it as a way of getting a week off.) Once I heard that they were keen to do it, it was a no-brainer. I realised I was putting myself under a bit of pressure, but if you play international cricket you're always under pressure, so it was no different really.

It was a very illuminating experience. I hadn't seen a lot of the young Somerset players and I was intrigued to know how a different county was run. I was very impressed by the whole Somerset set-up. They have a really good thing going on there, and that's shown in their consistency over recent years. A good ground at Taunton, great facilities and a culture that advocates many of the things that we look for in the England set-up – teamwork, hard work, fitness – and it's no surprise they've done well.

India looked a little jet-lagged, having just come from the West Indies. They seemed to be easing themselves into the tour, which for me was a great sign, because I'd been in England sides that had done that in the past, and you run the risk of going into the Test series undercooked. They were bowled out very cheaply on a flat wicket and didn't really get a chance to bat in the second innings. So I knew that there was an opportunity for us to exploit that in the first Test match at Lord's.

21–25 June, Lord's, 1st Test v India

We'd talked about taking things to a higher level against Sri Lanka. The most important thing before the India series was not to get distracted by the world rankings. It had long been a stated goal of ours to get to number one, but in the nuts and bolts of playing a series it was potentially dangerous for us to start thinking about that too far ahead.

We wanted to take the emotion out of it, almost take India out of it, and just concentrate on ourselves. We felt that with India it was important not to allow them to get on top; we also knew we had to be wary because they can sometimes appear very flat and not have much energy, yet they can take a wicket and suddenly their whole demeanour changes. So if we got on top of them, the plan was to make sure that we didn't let them come up for air; we had to finish them off.

We knew it was important for us not to drift away from what we'd done really well in Australia, which was not to let the enormity of the series cloud our judgement in the middle – not for one ball or over or session. It was a lesson we had learned as a side back in 2009 against Australia at Headingley. Before that game we had a players meeting and we were saying it's time to realise our dreams, one game and we've won the Ashes – all that sort of stuff. Sure enough, we were out of the game after the first session, probably because we weren't focusing on what was important, which was simply starting a game well. So ever since then, we've tried to make sure that doesn't happen again.

We knew that India would be vulnerable on wickets that nipped around, or if a ball was swinging a long way, so we asked the counties to produce wickets with a bit of grass on them if possible, and if there was some pace and carry that would be to our advantage as well. There were a couple of players we didn't know all that well, but for the big players, the likes of Dravid, Tendulkar, Laxman, we knew where their strengths and weaknesses were. We also knew they were very good players and were likely to get runs at some stage. But we would back our bowling attack against any batting line-up in the world, and we knew that if we bowled well, even those guys would struggle against us.

The match got off to the worst possible start. The first session in a series is very important for setting the tone; it can give one side early momentum. If you're in a boat race and the other crew get off to a faster start than you, you're behind them straight away and you have to work hard to catch up, or they might just disappear over the horizon. That morning it was very overcast, it was muggy, there was a green tinge to the wicket and we knew that it was going to be very hard to bat on – and we lost the toss and found ourselves up against prodigious seam and swing. At lunch we were very fortunate to be only one down. There had been plenty of playing-and-missing, and we felt we'd dodged a bullet. We weren't ahead in the series by any means, but we'd prevented them from getting off to a potentially very fast start.

They lost Zaheer Khan to injury on that first day. It was a massive moment for them because he's the lynchpin of their bowling attack. If he'd played throughout the series, the likes of Kumar and Sharma would have been a much harder proposition. But from that moment on there was always an outlet for scoring runs. If Zaheer had been there, he would have been threatening but also tight. From the other end, Kumar would have been tight and Sharma would have been threatening, so there would have been quite a good balance. As it was, he was a very hard man to replace. But I don't have any sympathy. You are dealt these things in cricket all the time, and you have to have a squad that's strong enough to cope with it.

It turned into a bit of a shemozzle. At one point, there was MS Dhoni taking his pads off and running in to bowl, and you could see them thinking this is ridiculous, we've got our keeper bowling and just look how unlucky we are. We knew that if we made 490, that was probably at least 100 or 150 above par, and although the Lord's wicket was flattening out we had a great opportunity to get a sizeable lead and go on to win the game.

Kevin Pietersen batted superbly for his 202. We're used to seeing KP play swashbuckling innings in which he dominates the bowling. For large periods of this innings he was very subdued; he had to leave well. He rode his luck a little but I thought it was a really mature performance from a top-quality player, and it underlined his great talent. The way he played Sharma in particular by going outside the line of off stump was impressive. He managed his game brilliantly in those conditions, and that's not something he's necessarily famed for.

When we bowled, Stuart Broad happily rediscovered his form. He had been coming under some pressure and hadn't bowled as well as he would have liked against Sri Lanka. I don't think he had a lot of luck, to be honest, but he didn't get any wickets, and as we all do, myself included in that series, he started questioning his methods a bit. And then there were all those 'enforcer' and 'he bowls too short' comments going round. I'd spoken to him about not buying into that 'enforcer' tag, and just banging out a length the way Anderson was, which he wasn't doing. There are circumstances in the game when you want to rough up the opposition, and he has a good bouncer and he can do that. But it shouldn't be his default. He got a wicket or two early on, which settled him down. He's always been a wicket-taking bowler and he always will be. We all go through fluctuations in form. The wicket had become a bit flatter, but our bowlers were able to get enough movement out of it to make life uncomfortable for the Indian batsmen. And from that point on we were in a great position to win the game.

In our second innings I think we were all conscious of the importance of grabbing the game by the scruff of the neck. It actually proved quite difficult to do; they were good at stopping us scoring and we found ourselves in a bit of trouble at 62–5. But Prior and Broad came out and the pendulum swung back in our favour. Prior's great strength is it's almost impossible to keep him quiet. If he's in for any length of time he's going to score quickly. You might get him out early, but if he sticks around he plays brilliantly. He's very unorthodox. He hits a lot between backward point and third man, which is hard to protect, and he disrupts the bowlers' length and line and mucks up the field settings in the same way that Gilchrist used to do when taking games away from the opposition.

We had to work very hard for that victory. We set them a vaguely achievable chase, though it was going to be hard work for them. The Lord's wicket is normally at its flattest on day five, and so it proved. At teatime we were still five wickets away from winning the game, so it looked as if they might salvage a draw, but our persistence finally paid off and it was great because we thoroughly deserved to win the game. There was some good resistance from Laxman and Raina and it wasn't easy, and none of us expected it to be so, but that makes it even more satisfying when you're able to win the match and take the lead in the series.

The only blot on our performance was our catching. Lord's is a hard ground to catch on. Particularly when it's overcast and swinging, the ball wobbles a lot. I dropped one off Laxman when the ball was coming straight at me and in the last yard it wobbled away, hitting me right on the end of the finger. You can't legislate for that; you see keepers dropping straightforward balls if they wobble. But in general it was a step down from our standards in the winter, when our fielding had been so outstanding, and it was something that we needed to address before the second Test, which was in only four days' time.

29 July–1 August, Trent Bridge, 2nd Test v India

In some ways Tim Bresnan coming in for the injured Tremlett for the second Test was a bit of a blessing in disguise. Our bowlers had had to work very hard to take those twenty Indian wickets at Lord's. Bresnan gave us a fresh pair of legs and someone who was likely to bowl well in the conditions at Trent Bridge – in fact, whenever he comes in he contributes, whether it's with the bat or the ball. So it was hard luck on Tremlett, who bowled brilliantly at Lord's, but there were certainly benefits to it.

We lost the toss again and had to bat in tough conditions. Again we were forced to battle very hard up to lunch, and this time we lost a lot of wickets. When Bell was out we were 124 for 8. But we showed one of the signs of a really good side by finding a way to get out of a bad position. It demonstrated our strength in depth. Numbers 7, 8, 9 and in this case 10 all have the ability to make life very difficult for opposition teams; they play positively, they take on the big shots, they force captains and scouts out everywhere and they run well between the wickets. We left it pretty late this time, but Swann and Broad came up with the goods and produced some outstanding counter-attacking batting.

It's a confidence thing. They feel that they're allowed to play their game and not conform to how Test match batsmen should necessarily play. Graeme Swann in particular always says, 'Don't give me any responsibility with the bat and I'll play well; if you give me responsibility I'll struggle.' They need that licence, and it's in our best interest to encourage them. We don't want them scratching around trying to get singles; we want them to whack the ball, and if they get out doing it, so be it. We shouldn't be in that position in the first place. It's not their fault.

You're still looking for awareness from them, of course, so if a batsman's nearing his hundred, or if there's a particularly dangerous bowler, then you expect them to try and hit at the other end. But we want them to go out and play their own game because I know personally how hard it is for opposition captains when sides bat like that. Suddenly your momentum can be taken away in the blink of an eye. In the course of thirty minutes you might see fifty runs squirted all over the place and your best bowlers getting whacked.

When India came in to bat, they had their best period of play in the series. The wicket was flat and they got to 250 for 4. We had every reason to expect them to go on and get a 150/200-run lead, which might have been impossible to overcome. Again, someone stood up and performed when it really mattered. We all realised that the second new ball was going to make or break the Test match, and it was Broad who produced one of the truly memorable moments, getting first

Yuvraj Singh, and then Dhoni, Harbhajan Singh and Kumar in a hat-trick in his next over. The game was turned completely on its head.

Then in our second innings came the Bell run-out incident. I saw it happen and my gut instinct was that it didn't look right. Bell wasn't trying to get a run – he was walking off for tea – and to be run out in those circumstances didn't feel right to me. There was consternation in the dressing room. Andy and I went into a separate room and said, 'Right, okay, what's the procedure from here, what can we do about it?' And we said, 'Well, the first thing we need to do is to clarify with the umpires what actually went on, was it the right decision that he was run out?' The umpires said that by the strict letter of the law he was out. They said the only way he could be reinstated was if India withdrew their appeal, and they'd given them the opportunity to do that a couple of times but they hadn't taken it. So in those circumstances I felt that it was worthwhile speaking to MS Dhoni and just saying that we think you should consider withdrawing your appeal.

I went to the Indian dressing room to have a word with him and Duncan Fletcher, the Indian coach. I was concerned not to put them under undue pressure, because it wasn't my call at the end of the day. I just said that I didn't think it felt right. I thought it could potentially hinder the relationship between the two sides for the rest of the series, which up to then had been excellent. I said that as captains we don't get many opportunities to lead the game in the right way, and that this was possibly one of those opportunities, but I did stress that it was his call. Dhoni said he would think about it and see what the players had to say.

The next thing, the umpires had gone out and there was quite a long delay while the Indians mulled it over in the dressing room. We had the next batsman ready to go in but Bell was still padded up too. Then the word came up that they'd withdrawn their appeal. I think it was the right decision. In fact, it was a brave decision for Dhoni to make because I know what it's like when emotions are running high: sometimes you aren't able to look at the bigger picture. I was in that situation once in South Africa in the Champions Trophy when I had to call a Sri Lankan batsman back after a collision, and I wasn't popular with my team-mates for a while. But when you have time to look back on it without the competitive juices flowing you can see that there are benefits. It sets a precedent for other captains. (The next morning I went up to Dhoni and thanked him for withdrawing the appeal and he said, 'Well, just make sure it doesn't happen again.')

After that, however, the Indians seemed to fall apart. Suddenly, having been completely behind, we were in an unassailable position and had a great opportunity to finish the game. We were held up a little by Sachin Tendulkar. He got a fifty but he didn't have that nice controlled tempo you usually see. He was going at the ball quite hard. I tended to put Anderson on whenever he came in. His record against him is tremendous. He has a lot of ways of getting Tendulkar out. He brings the stumps into play and in seaming conditions he's difficult if you go at the ball with quite a big stride, as Tendulkar was doing. I don't think he was burdened by the expectation of making his hundredth hundred. He was just struggling against high-quality bowling. He never looked as secure as normal.

Bresnan contributed dramatically again with five wickets in their second innings. This was his eighth Test and his eighth victory., He's repeatedly demonstrated how under-rated he was twelve or eighteen months ago. He's now got confidence and he's a very talented cricketer. He can swing it, he bowls heavy balls, he can reverse it well and his batting is very strong for a number 8 batsman.

We spent a couple of hours in the dressing room after we'd secured the 319-run victory, as we always do. We obviously felt we were in a great position to go on and win the series, being 2–0 up with two to play. We were very close to achieving our goal and becoming number one, but we were determined to remain focused on the hard work still to be done. Edgbaston was going to be crucial.

I'm sure at times during that Trent Bridge game India were thinking it was going to be 1–1 in the series heading to Birmingham, but suddenly it was 2–0 and the series had pretty much slipped from their grasp. Their bowlers had bowled a lot of overs and were getting very tired. A few of their batsmen were getting scores, but the only guy who was really standing up for them was Dravid, and you can't win a series with one batsman.

10–13 August, Edgbaston, 3rd Test v India

Two days before the game we were up in our hotel looking down on the city centre of Birmingham and all we could see were police lights flashing left, right and centre. There was a lot of noise and we were thinking that it was actually getting quite serious; the rioting seemed to be spreading and getting worse and worse. Come Tuesday morning, there was a lot of chat about whether the game should go ahead and whether the Indians were feeling safe. This was just a game of cricket at a time when our country was not going through one of its finest hours. In the end, we were quite comfortable with the game being played as long as the security could be guaranteed, but it was one of those instances when you were aware that something bigger was going on in the world and that what we were doing on a cricket field was pretty insignificant.

In the event, when we turned up on the Wednesday morning for the start of the game there was a massive pillar of smoke coming from an industrial warehouse down the road. It turned out to be nothing to do with the riots, but it kept everyone on their toes; the challenge in those circumstances is to make sure that you're focusing on the cricket and nothing else.

We won the toss and bowled and the wicket actually

played better than we thought it would. It was very green but it played okay. Fortunately we managed to get two or three wickets just before lunch. Sehwag had come back into their side, but it was always going to be tough for him to come straight in, having not played for a number of months, and he received a good ball first up and suddenly their supposed saviour was back in the pavilion. It gave us great momentum to knock them over once again for a lowish score.

Then Alastair Cook took over. He'd struggled in the series up to that point, having had an amazing run before that, but this time he got in and was determined to make the most of it. The most impressive thing about his innings was its steady pace. He got to 100 and he just kept playing the same way. He was very patient against the spinner and he left well. When he got to 150 and then 200 he just carried on. He batted for an incredible length of time but there were no lapses in concentration, no sudden impulses to whack the ball over the bowler's head – there was no change. The best players are able to do that, just keep playing the same way. We've seen Trott do it time and time again, and Cook's so clear in his method these days that he doesn't feel the need to go outside of it. It was absolutely gutting for him not to get that 300. You don't get many opportunities to do that in your career and you can see he was distraught.

I remember when he came in for lunch after the third morning, he had scored over 200 and he'd used the same gloves for the whole twelve hours, as well as practising with them in the morning. When Anderson put them on they were stone-dry; there was not one drop of sweat in them. It was just freakish. And it really did demonstrate that he does not sweat – or that he was finding his batting so easy that sweating wasn't necessary. It was an immense feat of concentration and I'm sure even Goochie would have been happy if he'd gone on and got past that 333.

We eventually made 710 for 7, which really underlined our increasing dominance. I had felt the same thing happen against Australia. Two reasonably evenly matched sides at the start, but over the course of the series our confidence increased while theirs decreased and by the end there was quite a wide margin between the sides. The Indian bowlers had bowled thousands of overs, they were tired and they weren't getting any wickets. They were probably frustrated with their batsmen for not getting bigger scores and you could see them getting into that situation where you feel as if you've got nowhere to run and hide.

What pleased me most about the Edgbaston performance was that we ground them down and they weren't able to recover. A lot of teams would have been very happy with 500 in those circumstances. The fact that we were able to get 700 and completely destroy any hope they might have of winning the Test match, or even drawing it, was a good demonstration of ruthlessness, which is crucial at the highest level.

Just as we were finishing our mammoth first innings,

Broad said, 'I've had a vision. Sehwag's getting a king pair; he's going to nick it to you at first slip, first ball.' It's one of the most sensible things Broad has ever said. Our plans for Sehwag generally were to be very straight, but in that circumstance Anderson said to me, 'Look, first ball I'm going to give him the opportunity to play the shot through the off side and put it out a little wider,' and I said that was perfect because there was likely to be a bit of swing there. He got it spot on. Sehwag went for the shot and got the nick and I took the catch!

Anderson was outstanding again. He got Gambhir and Dravid, then Laxman with an absolute jaffa. It's down to relentlessly putting every ball in the right area plus a little bit of movement. He can't be praised highly enough. He has amazing versatility in the way he can bowl inswingers and outswingers at will and remain incredibly accurate and get some movement off the pitch as well. He's three bowlers in one. He can play a number of different roles. He's the attacking bowler with the new ball; in the middle he sometimes just sits in and says right, I'm going to build up pressure, you get the wickets at the other end; and then, if a left-hander's in, he can bowl round the wicket like a left-arm-over bowler.

We took the last wicket just after lunch on the fourth day. We had won the series and achieved our goal of reaching number one in the world. That was right up there with winning the Ashes. Edgbaston has a huge cavernous dressing room now. It's an amazing facility but it can be slightly difficult to get that close togetherness there, that intimacy, but there was some real emotion on this occasion. I felt very emotional because we'd been on a long journey to get to number one in the world, and everyone had put in so much hard work and graft, and we'd achieved it a lot quicker than we thought we would.

We all felt it was a hugely significant time in our careers, achieving a lofty goal, something no England side had really achieved for forty years or so. It was one of those moments I'll remember very sharply in my mind. And it allowed us some time to think about not just the eleven that were there but all those who had helped us on that journey as well, the likes of Collingwood and Onions and all the others who had played such an important part.

Andy and I both made speeches. I certainly felt incredible pride in what each individual member – not just the team but the back-up staff as well – had put into achieving the goals we'd set. It's not often you get a chance to look back at what you've done and how far you've come, to appreciate the sheer graft that people have put into it, whether it's the analyst or the physio or the fitness conditioning coach or the players themselves. One of the points I made was that each of us knows just how much hard work we've put into this. It's not just what happens on the pitch; it's what happens away from the pitch, practising or at the gym, and we do it for these moments. A lot of good players put in a lot of hard work and don't get that reward, and we have been very fortunate.

18–22 August, The Oval, 4th Test v India

The fourth Test was just the icing on the cake. A lot of sides have struggled when they've already won a series to have the ruthlessness to win again, but we were excellent in that match. The pitch turned a bit and Graeme Swann underlined his importance to the side. We had to graft pretty hard, but it was enjoyable graft in the sense that we weren't under any real pressure; the series was already won and we just had to make sure we remained hungry enough to finish them off. Strong bowling won us the game again. It was a fitting end to an outstanding series, one in which we had taken things to the next level. Our batting was stronger than it had ever been before; our bowling maintained its high standards.

Tendulkar got close to his coveted hundredth hundred in that match before getting out for 91. In some ways it didn't feel right for him to get it in those circumstances, a dead rubber at the end of a series in which they'd been beaten comfortably. It just didn't seem to be the proper environment for him to be achieving that milestone.

The more I look back on it, the more I'm surprised that we've reached the top of the rankings as quickly as we have. To do it in the space of just over two years is a mammoth effort. In some ways, it underlines the importance of not seeing this as the finishing point; you can't go from a run-of-the-mill Test side to number one in the world in two and a half years, and then imagine you've cracked it.

We've obviously made improvements, but there hasn't been time for the culture to set in strongly enough to carry us through for another four or five years. That's the challenge now. We haven't played any Test cricket in the subcontinent recently. Just as winning in Australia was a bit of a Holy Grail for us, so our attention must now turn to winning in those conditions. To build a legacy, we need to be able to win all over the world, and win consistently.

I saw an interview with Gary Neville talking about the England football team. He was highlighting the fact that the cricket team had been able to move from worrying about the pressure of performing to actually performing, because we were confident enough to do it. When you hear people from other sports looking to what we've done as an example, that makes you feel as if you're on the right track. So often in the past it's been us looking to other sports for inspiration. It's encouraging that they are looking in our direction now.

We've had a pretty much unbroken run of success for a while now. My ethos on captaincy is that, with the best will in the world, you're not going to win things without good players. Having said that, what I am proudest about is the environment we've created. It's not the decision you make out in the middle when the team are 100 for 5 or what you decide to do with the toss that's important. What matters is getting the best out of the players you have. I think we've done that. And I actually think the players themselves have been surprised by how good they really are. Maybe in the past we haven't had that belief.

Over the course of two years we've managed to instil that belief. Not always by design, sometimes by accident, we've managed to create a huge bond between the players and to encourage an atmosphere in which players are not afraid to look to be the best in the world. There is no fear, and we've engendered the idea of playing for each other rather than just for yourself, the idea of challenging yourselves to be better than anyone else in the world. Why should Jacques Kallis be better than us? Why should Ricky Ponting be better than us? Why should Sachin Tendulkar be better than us? Sometimes you have to raise your expectations. And if you do that, you'll be surprised how far you can go.

It's a matter of raising your game as an individual, but for the team benefit as well as your own benefit. That takes a bit of pressure off yourself. Imagine you're standing there saying, 'I'm going to average 57; that means I need to get this number of runs.' If instead you just put yourself in the moment and say, 'The team needs me to get runs here today,' then you don't think about all that other stuff. You just deal with what you encounter on the pitch.

There's no hierarchal system in our side. The support staff are recognised as having huge value. So, it's not just Huw Bevan telling me to do a weight session. His role is to help us perform in the middle, and he's not doing things for the sake of it. If he thinks it's going to help, he'll suggest it and players will get on with it. If he doesn't think it's going to help, he won't mention it.

One of the best things Andy Flower has done, out of a multitude of great things, is that he's managed the management brilliantly. So they're very respectful of the players having to go out there and perform. They don't just throw stuff down your throat all the time; they have a filtering process among themselves before it reaches the players. And Andy himself has been the embodiment of challenging ourselves. He's constantly pushing players not to rest on their laurels, to improve, and he does it in a way that is not threatening but encouraging. The respect he's held in by the team can't be underestimated. He's been the fulcrum around which everything else has worked.

However hard or desperate you are to chase your dreams on a cricket field, a sense of perspective is crucial. And sitting back here at home, I realise my kids don't care if I'm an Ashes-winning captain or the captain of the best team in the world; they care about the fact that I'm their dad. And I think that's a healthy thing; it allows you not to be disheartened when things don't go your way, and not to get too carried away when you do well.

Sri Lanka in England 2011

Tests

1st Test. SWALEC Stadium, Cardiff. 26–30 May 2011
Sri Lanka 400 (H.A.P.W. Jayawardene 112) and 82 (G.P. Swann 4–16, C.T. Tremlett 4–40)
England 496–5 dec (I.J.L. Trott 203, A.N. Cook 133, I.R. Bell 103*)
England won by an innings and 14 runs

2nd Test. Lord's, London. 3–7 June 2011
England 486 (M.J. Prior 126, A.N. Cook 96) and 335–7 dec (A.N. Cook 106, K.P. Pietersen 72)
Sri Lanka 479 (T.M. Dilshan 193, N.T. Paranavitana 65) and 127–3
Match drawn

3rd Test. The Rose Bowl, Southampton. 16–20 June 2011
Sri Lanka 184 (H.A.P.W. Jayawardene 43, C.T. Tremlett 6–48) and 334–5 (K.C. Sangakkara 119, T.T. Samaraweera 87*)
England 377–8 dec (I.R. Bell 119*, K.P. Pietersen 85)
Match drawn

England won the series 1–0.

India in England 2011

Tests – The Pataudi Trophy

1st Test. Lord's, London. 21–25 July 2011
England 474–8 dec (K.P. Pietersen 202, M.J. Prior 71, I.J.L. Trott 70, P. Kumar 5–106) and 269–6 dec (M.J. Prior 103*)
India 286 (R. Dravid 103*, S.C.J. Broad 4–37) and 261 (S.K. Raina 78, V.V.S. Laxman 56, J.M. Anderson 5–65)
England won by 196 runs

2nd Test.Trent Bridge, Nottingham. 29 July–1 August 2011
England 221 (S.C.J. Broad 64) and 544 (I.R. Bell 159, T.T. Bresnan 90)
India 288 (R. Dravid 117, Yuvraj Singh 62, S.C.J Broad 6–46) and 158 (S.R. Tendulkar 56, T.T. Bresnan 5–48)
England won by 319 runs

3rd Test. Edgbaston, Birmingham. 10–13 August 2011
India 224 (M.S. Dhoni 77, S.C.J. Broad 4–53, T.T. Bresnan 4–62) and 244 (M.S. Dhoni 74*, J.M. Anderson 4–85)
England 710–7 dec (A.N. Cook 294, E.J.G. Morgan 104, A.J. Strauss 87)
England won by an innings and 242 runs

4th Test. The Oval, London. 18–22 August 2011
England 591–6 dec (I.R. Bell 235, K.P. Pietersen 175)
India 300 (R. Dravid 146*) and 283 (f/o) (S.R. Tendulkar 91, A. Mishra 84, G.P. Swann 6–106)
England won by an innings and 8 runs

England won the series 4–0.

21

THE ASHES 2010–11
ENGLAND PLAYER
PROFILES

*Up to and including Fifth Test
v Australia at Sydney*

Alastair Cook

Ashes 2010–11 Record

	M	Inns	NO	Runs	HS	Avge	SR	100	50	Ct	St
Batting	5	7	1	766	235*	127.66	53.26	3	2	5	-

Test Match Career Record 2006–2011

	M	Inns	NO	Runs	HS	Avge	100	50	Ct	St
Batting	65	115	7	5130	235*	47.50	16	24	57	-

Came of age as an England player on the tour of Australia. An absolutely immense presence at the top of the order, scoring more runs in an Ashes series for England than anyone apart from Wally Hammond. The fifth highest runs in an Ashes series ever, earning his nickname, The Don. Incredibly consistent on the pitch and a great source of help and encouragement in a team that look upon him as a confidant. Amazingly committed cricketer; very fit, doesn't sweat, so brilliant in hot weather, and in charge of reverse swing and general care of the ball. No one does more for the England cricket team than him. But he's not one to look for the accolades. Runs like a bloke who's chasing a bus with a walking stick. Bears a remarkable likeness to Woody from *Toy Story* in the way he walks and carries his limbs.

Jonathan Trott

Ashes 2010–11 Record

	Mat	Inns	NO	Runs	HS	Avge	SR	100	50	Ct	St
Batting	5	7	2	445	168*	89.00	50.39	2	1	1	-

Test Match Career Record 2009–2011

	M	Inns	NO	Runs	HS	Avge	100	50	Ct	St
Batting	18	30	4	1600	226	61.53	5	5	9	-

Becoming the top number three batsman in the world, with the best average in that position for England since Ted Dexter. An unbelievably unflustered batsman. Once he gets in the zone, is incredibly hard to dismiss. Fielding has improved dramatically over the two years he's been with the side. His no-nonsense attitude to the game of cricket, added to his colourful language in the dressing room, has been a breath of fresh air. Marks his guard incessantly (even when the match is over). His obsessive nature is equally evident off the pitch with his amazing addiction/dedication to gaming in general. FIFA, Call of Duty, Tiger Woods, Angry Birds – anything that can be played on an electronic gadget will have his undivided attention for hours on end.

Kevin Pietersen

Ashes 2010–11 Record

	Mat	Inns	NO	Runs	HS	Avge	SR	100	50	Ct	St
Batting	5	6	0	360	227	60.00	63.94	1	1	5	-

	Overs	Mdns	Runs	Wkts	Avge	Econ	SR	BBI	BBM	5wI	10wM
Bowling	5.0	0	16	1	16.00	3.20	30.0	1/10	1/10	-	-

Test Match Career Record 2005–2011

	M	Inns	NO	Runs	HS	Avge	100	50	Ct	St
Batting	71	123	6	5666	227	48.42	17	21	44	-

	M	Balls	RC	Wkts	Avge	RPO	BB	5I	10M
Bowling	71	873	584	5	116.80	4.01	1-0	-	-

Brilliant player looked up to not only by our players but by players around the world. Instrumental in us winning the Ashes in 2005, and the only player to master the Australian conditions in 2006–07. Came into the 2010–11 series under a bit of pressure and struggling to perform. Proved his class with his amazing double century at Adelaide. Has incredibly good work ethic. Very meticulous, one of three or four in our dressing room we call 'beavers'. They have to have everything just so before a Test match starts – bats in line, gloves numbered, trainers and cricket shoes in the right spot. Not quite as obsessive about it as Jonathan Trott, but close. Slightly unhealthy addiction to Red Bull and Twitter.

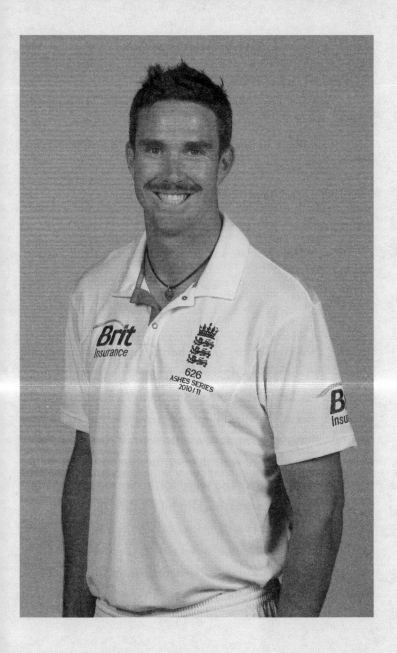

Paul Collingwood

Ashes 2010–11 Record

	Mat	Inns	NO	Runs	HS	Avge	SR	100	50	Ct	St
Batting	5	6	0	83	42	13.83	46.62	-	-	9	-

	Overs	Mdns	Runs	Wkts	Avge	Econ	SR	BBI	BBM	5wI	10wM
Bowling	31.0	6	73	2	36.50	2.35	93.0	1/3	1/5	-	-

Test Match Career Record 2003–2011

	M	Inns	NO	Runs	HS	Avge	100	50	Ct	St
Batting	68	115	10	4259	206	40.56	10	20	96	-

	M	Balls	RC	Wkts	Avge	RPO	BB	5I	10M
Bowling	68	1905	1018	17	59.88	3.20	3-23	-	-

The old campaigner, the guy who's seemingly been around for ever, a real stalwart for English cricket in both one-day and Test cricket, a valuable source of advice for me on the pitch. Lives and breathes England cricket, while retaining a very healthy determination to enjoy every moment. Consistently up there with the best fielders in the world for the last decade. Called The Weed for his incredibly wiry and feeble physique. Lowest backlift in world cricket. But has definitely squeezed every ounce out of the abilities he's been given, to the great benefit of others. Always up, always bubbly, can't sit still for a moment. Pretty decent on the golf course until he lost his swing halfway through the tour.

Ian Bell

Ashes 2010–11 Record

	Mat	Inns	NO	Runs	HS	Avge	SR	100	50	Ct	St
Batting	5	6	1	329	115	65.80	56.14	1	3	3	-

Test Match Career Record 2004–2011

	M	Inns	NO	Runs	HS	Avge	100	50	Ct	St
Batting	62	106	11	4192	199	44.12	12	26	53	-

The quiet achiever. Most stylish batsman in the team. In the last two years he's taken his game to a new level by working out his method and by maturing and taking on more responsibility. Great hundred in Sydney. Very good cricket brain, often comes out with suggestions on the pitch. A guy with an incredible work ethic, always first at the ground and in the nets. Used to be a bit of a practical joker, famed for his chirpiness after a few beers. These days much more serious and focused on what he needs to do.

Matt Prior

Ashes 2010–11 Record

	Mat	Inns	NO	Runs	HS	Avge	SR	100	50	Ct	St
Batting	5	6	1	252	118	50.40	78.26	1	1	23	-

Test Match Career Record 2007–2011

	M	Inns	NO	Runs	HS	Avge	100	50	Ct	St
Batting	40	61	11	2148	131*	42.96	4	16	117	4

Mr Immaculate, almost Alec Stewart II. Always perfectly turned out, always has his sweatbands in the right place and his collars fully starched. An incredibly powerful presence behind the stumps for both the bowlers and the fielders; very much the fulcrum around which our fielding unit works. World-class keeper, very dangerous attacking batsman and a very good cricket brain. Absolutely determined to make the most of his reincarnation as an England cricketer. Funny in the dressing room, has important role as a go-between for the young, slightly prima donna-ish bowlers and the serious, slightly more switched-on batsmen. Nicknamed Cheese because if something looks cheesy, he'll probably be wearing it.

Tim Bresnan

Ashes 2010–11 Record

	Mat	Inns	NO	Runs	HS	Avge	SR	100	50	Ct	St
Batting	2	2	0	39	35	19.50	32.50	-	-	-	-

	Overs	Mdns	Runs	Wkts	Avge	Econ	SR	BBI	BBM	5wI	10wM
Bowling	82.4	25	215	11	19.54	2.60	45.0	4/50	6/75	-	-

Test Match Career Record 2009–2011

	M	Inns	NO	Runs	HS	Avge	100	50	Ct	St
Batting	7	5	0	164	91	32.80	-	1	3	-

	M	Balls	RC	Wkts	Avge	RPO	BB	5I	10M
Bowling	7	1482	707	25	28.28	2.86	4-50	-	-

Mr Dependable, with a great no-nonsense Yorkshire attitude to the game. Known as Breslad. Much underrated as a bowler prior to the series. Has great control over the ball. Very skilful reverse swing bowler, and hugely reliable member of the team. Plays to his strengths, which are accuracy and a bit of bounce. Appreciates his role in the side, not interested in being a big star. Invaluable. Handles being the regular butt of Swann and Anderson's jokes, usually relating to his physique, very well.

Stuart Broad

Ashes 2010–11 Record

	Mat	Inns	NO	Runs	HS	Avge	SR	100	50	Ct	St
Batting	2	1	0	0	0	0.00	0.00	-	-	-	-

	Overs	Mdns	Runs	Wkts	Avge	Econ	SR	BBI	BBM	5wI	10wM
Bowling	69.5	17	161	2	80.50	2.30	209.5	1/18	1/71	-	-

Test Match Career Record 2007–2010

	M	Inns	NO	Runs	HS	Avge	100	50	Ct	St
Batting	34	46	6	1096	169	27.40	1	5	9	-

	M	Balls	RC	Wkts	Avge	RPO	BB	5I	10M
Bowling	34	6693	3489	99	35.24	3.12	6-91	3	-

Blue-eyed boy of the England cricket team. Very talented, very clear sense of what his strengths are and how to use them. Possesses possibly the best bouncer in world cricket. Has a refreshingly honest view of the game and is intelligent thinker on it. Always assessing the conditions. Missed him massively once he was injured in the second Test. Big pals with Matt Prior and shares slightly unhealthy fascination with his appearance; while others are loosening up in the changing rooms, he's doing his hair.

Graeme Swann

Ashes 2010–11 Record

	Mat	Inns	NO	Runs	HS	Avge	SR	100	50	Ct	St
Batting	5	5	1	88	36*	22.00	88.88	-	-	6	-

	Overs	Mdns	Runs	Wkts	Avge	Econ	SR	BBI	BBM	5wI	10wM
Bowling	219.1	43	597	15	39.80	2.72	87.6	5/91	7/161	1	-

Test Match Career Record 2008–2011

	M	Inns	NO	Runs	HS	Avge	100	50	Ct	St
Batting	29	36	6	741	85	24.70	-	4	25	-

	M	Balls	RC	Wkts	Avge	RPO	BB	5I	10M
Bowling	29	7431	3598	128	28.10	2.90	6-65	10	1

Team buffoon. Has an amazing ability to regurgitate movie lines, song lines, mimic people's accents and generally lighten the mood. Plays a huge role in the side in not taking life too seriously. A phenomenal bowler who's asked questions of just about every batsman that's come up against him. Very competitive, feisty performer, takes enormous pride in his own performance. Leader of the team song and Sprinkler Dance and still maintains that cricket is just a sideshow for him until his proper career as an all-round entertainer starts. But very superstitious and gave up guitar and golf on tour for fear that it might affect our results.

James Anderson

Ashes 2010–11 Record

	Mat	Inns	NO	Runs	HS	Avge	SR	100	50	Ct	St
Batting	5	5	0	22	11	4.40	26.50	-	-	4	-

	Overs	Mdns	Runs	Wkts	Avge	Econ	SR	BBI	BBM	5wI	10wM
Bowling	213.1	50	625	24	26.04	2.93	53.2	4/44	7/127	-	-

Test Match Career Record 2003–2011

	M	Inns	NO	Runs	HS	Avge	100	50	Ct	St
Batting	57	76	31	524	34	11.64	-	-	25	-

	M	Balls	RC	Wkts	Avge	RPO	BB	5I	10M
Bowling	57	12056	6595	212	31.10	3.28	7-43	10	1

Mr Grumpy, in common with many fast bowlers. The leader of our bowling attack; has amazing skills with a swinging ball. Developed hugely as a bowler in the last three or four years, transforming from the young tearaway to the ruthless assassin who gets the most out of every wicket he encounters. Performed brilliantly in the Ashes, taking many vital wickets, including Ponting three times early on. Also one of our best fielders. Major natural ability in just about every sport. Very much Graeme Swann's sidekick. Fairly laid-back character in the dressing room who spends most of his time thinking of new ways of taking the mickey out of Tim Bresnan. Surprisingly good at crosswords.

Chris Tremlett

Ashes 2010–11 Record

	Mat	Inns	NO	Runs	HS	Avge	SR	100	50	Ct	St
Batting	3	4	1	19	12	6.33	36.53	-	-	-	-

	Overs	Mdns	Runs	Wkts	Avge	Econ	SR	BBI	BBM	5wI	10wM
Bowling	122.3	28	397	17	23.35	3.24	43.2	5/87	8/150	1	-

Test Match Career Record 2007–2011

	M	Inns	NO	Runs	HS	Avge	100	50	Ct	St
Batting	6	9	2	69	25*	9.85	-	-	1	-

	M	Balls	RC	Wkts	Avge	RPO	BB	5I	10M
Bowling	6	1594	783	30	26.10	2.94	5-87	1	-

Vastly different player to the one I first encountered. Seemed a bit soft then; now very assured about his own game. Very skilful bowler with quiet, relaxed ruthlessness that surprised and impressed everyone on tour. Had a massive impact when he came into the team and bowled superbly. An avid music listener; never find him without his headphones on. His size and his appearance combine in an amazing ability to turn heads when walking down a street.

Steve Finn

Ashes 2010–11 Record

	Mat	Inns	NO	Runs	HS	Avge	SR	100	50	Ct	St
Batting	3	3	2	3	2	3.00	37.50	-	-	2	-

	Overs	Mdns	Runs	Wkts	Avge	Econ	SR	BBI	BBM	5wI	10wM
Bowling	107.4	9	464	14	33.14	4.30	46.1	6/125	6/150	1	-

Test Match Career Record 2010

	M	Inns	NO	Runs	HS	Avge	100	50	Ct	St
Batting	11	12	9	16	9*	5.33	-	-	3	-

	M	Balls	RC	Wkts	Avge	RPO	BB	5I	10M
Bowling	11	1828	1207	46	26.23	3.96	6-125	3	-

The youngest member of the side. Bears a striking resemblance to an Avatar. A brilliant character to have in your side. Very confident bloke, not afraid to voice his opinions. Works hard, learns every day and has all the raw materials to become one of the great England fast bowlers. In addition to the natural asset of his height, he hits the deck hard, reverse-swings the ball well and has a very solid and repeatable action. Over the course of the Ashes learnt a huge amount about bowling away from home. Along with Bresnan, was the main recipient of Swann and Anderson's jokes both on and off the Twittersphere, mostly because of his north London gangster talk, even though he's from a solid middle-class family.

THE ASHES 2010−11
SCORECARDS

AUSTRALIA v ENGLAND
(1st Test)

At Brisbane 25-29 November 2010

ENGLAND

*A.J.Strauss c Hussey b Hilfenhaus	0	- st Haddin b North	110
A.N.Cook c Watson b Siddle	67	- not out	235
I.J.L.Trott b Watson	29	- not out	135
K.P.Pietersen c Ponting b Siddle	43		
P.D.Collingwood c North b Siddle	4		
I.R.Bell c Watson b Doherty	76		
+M.J.Prior b Siddle	0		
S.C.J.Broad lbw b Siddle	0		
G.P.Swann lbw b Siddle	10		
J.M.Anderson b Doherty	11		
S.T.Finn not out	0		
l-b 8, w 7, n-b 5	20	B 17, l-b 4, w 10, n-b 6	37
	----		----
1/0 2/41 3/117 4/125 5/197	260	1/188	(for 1 wkt dec) 517
6/197 7/197 8/228 9/254 10/260			

Bowling: *First innings* - Hilfenhaus 19-4-60-1; Siddle 16-3-54-6; Johnson 15-2-66-0; Watson 12-2-30-1; Doherty 13.5-3-41-2; North 1-0-1-0. *Second innings* - Hilfenhaus 32-8-82-0; Siddle 24-4-90-0; North 19-3-47-1; Johnson 27-5-104-0; Doherty 35-5-107-0; Watson 15-2-66-0.

AUSTRALIA

S.R.Watson c Strauss b Anderson	36	- not out	41
S.M.Katich c and b Finn	50	- c Strauss b Broad	4
*R.T.Ponting c Prior b Anderson	10	- not out	51
M.J.Clarke c Prior b Finn	9		
M.E.K.Hussey c Cook b Finn	195		
M.J.North c Collingwood b Swann	1		
+B.J.Haddin c Collingwood b Swann	136		
M.G.Johnson b Finn	0		
X.J.Doherty c Cook b Finn	16		
P.M.Siddle c Swann b Finn	6		
B.W.Hilfenhaus not out	1		
B 4, l-b 12, w 4, n-b 1	21	B 4, l-b 1, w 1, pens 5	11
	----		----
1/78 2/96 3/100 4/140 5/143	481	1/5	(for 1 wkt) 107
6/450 7/458 8/462 9/472 10/481			

Bowling: *First innings* – Anderson 37-13-99-2; Broad 33-7-72-0; Swann 43-5-128-2; Finn 33.4-1-125-6; Collingwood 12-1-41-0. *Second innings* - Anderson 5-2-15-0; Broad 7-1-18-1; Swann 8-0-33-0; Finn 4-0-25-0; Pietersen 2-0-6-0.

Umpires: Aleem Dar and B.R.Doctrove

Match drawn

AUSTRALIA v ENGLAND
(2nd Test)

At Adelaide 3-7 December 2010

AUSTRALIA

S.R.Watson c Pietersen b Anderson	51	- c Strauss b Finn	57
S.M.Katich run out (Trott)	0	- c Prior b Swann	43
*R.T.Ponting c Swann b Anderson	0	- c Collingwood b Swann	9
M.J.Clarke c Swann b Anderson	2	- c Cook b Pietersen	80
M.E.K.Hussey c Collingwood b Swann	93	- c Anderson b Finn	52
M.J.North c Prior b Finn	26	- lbw b Swann	22
+B.J.Haddin c Finn b Broad	56	- c Prior b Anderson	12
R.J.Harris lbw b Swann	0	- lbw b Anderson	0
X.J.Doherty run out (Strauss/Cook/Prior)	6	- b Swann	5
P.M.Siddle c Cook b Anderson	3	- b Swann	6
D.E.Bollinger not out	0	- not out	7
l-b 6, w 1, n-b 1	8	B 5, l-b 1, w 5	11

1/0 2/0 3/2 4/96 5/156   245   1/84 2/98 3/134 4/238 5/261   304
6/207 7/207 8/226 9/243 10/245   6/286 7/286 8/286 9/295 10/304

Bowling: *First innings* - Anderson 19-4-51-4; Broad 18.5-6-39-1; Finn 16-1-71-1; Swann 29-2-70-2; Collingwood 3-0-8-0.

Second innings - Anderson 22-4-92-2; Broad 11-3-32-0; Swann 41.1-12-91-5; Finn 18-2-60-2; Collingwood 4-0-13-0; Pietersen 3-0-10-1.

ENGLAND

*A.J.Strauss b Bollinger	1
A.N.Cook c Haddin b Harris	148
I.J.L.Trott c Clarke b Harris	78
K.P.Pietersen c Katich b Doherty	227
P.D.Collingwood lbw b Watson	42
I.R.Bell not out	68
+M.J.Prior not out	27
S.C.J.Broad	
G.P.Swann	
J.M.Anderson	
S.T.Finn	
B 8, l-b 13, w 8	29

1/3 2/176 3/351 4/452   (for 5 wkts dec) 620
5/568

Bowling: *First innings* - Harris 29-5-84-2; Bollinger 29-1-130-1; Siddle 30-3-121-0; Watson 19-7-44-1; Doherty 27-3-158-1; North 18-0-62-0.

Umpires: M.Erasmus and A.L.Hill

England won by an innings and 71 runs

AUSTRALIA v ENGLAND
(3rd Test)

At Perth 16-19 December 2010

AUSTRALIA

S.R.Watson lbw b Finn	13	- lbw b Tremlett	95
P.J.Hughes b Tremlett	2	- c Collingwood b Finn	12
*R.T.Ponting c Collingwood b Anderson	12	- c Prior b Finn	1
M.J.Clarke c Prior b Tremlett	4	- b Tremlett	20
M.E.K.Hussey c Prior b Swann	61	- c Swann b Tremlett	116
S.P.D.Smith c Strauss b Tremlett	7	- c Prior b Tremlett	36
+B.J.Haddin c Swann b Anderson	53	- b Tremlett	7
M.G.Johnson c Anderson b Finn	62	- c Bell b Collingwood	1
R.J.Harris b Anderson	3	- c Bell b Finn	1
P.M.Siddle not out	35	- c Collingwood b Anderson	8
B.W.Hilfenhaus c Cook b Swann	13	- not out	0
l-b 3	3	l-b 6, w 4, n-b 2	12
	----		----
1/2 2/17 3/28 4/36 5/69	268	1/31 2/34 3/64 4/177 5/252	309
6/137 7/189 8/201 9/233 10/268		6/271 7/276 8/284 9/308 10/309	

Bowling: *First innings* - Anderson 20-3-61-3; Tremlett 23-3-63-3; Finn 15-1-86-2; Collingwood 2-0-3-0; Swann 16-0-52-2. *Second innings* - Anderson 26-7-65-1; Tremlett 24-4-87-5; Finn 21-4-97-3; Swann 9-0-51-0; Collingwood 6-3-3-1.

ENGLAND

*A.J.Strauss c Haddin b Harris	52	- c Ponting b Johnson	15
A.N.Cook c Hussey b Johnson	32	- lbw b Harris	13
I.J.L.Trott lbw b Johnson	4	- c Haddin b Johnson	31
K.P.Pietersen lbw b Johnson	0	- c Watson b Hilfenhaus	3
P.D.Collingwood lbw b Johnson	5	- c Smith b Harris	11
I.R.Bell c Ponting b Harris	53	(7) lbw b Harris	16
+M.J.Prior b Siddle	12	(8) c Hussey b Harris	10
G.P.Swann c Haddin b Harris	11	(9) b Johnson	9
C.T.Tremlett b Johnson	2	(10) not out	1
J.M.Anderson c Watson b Johnson	0	(6) b Harris	3
S.T.Finn not out	1	- c Smith b Harris	2
B 8, l-b 4, w 1, n-b 2	15	l-b 8, n-b 1	9
	----		----
1/78 2/82 3/82 4/94	187	1/23 2/37 3/55 4/81 5/81	123
5/98 6/145 7/181 8/186 9/186 10/187		6/94 7/111 8/114 9/120 10/123	

Bowling: *First innings* – Hilfenhaus 21-6-53-0; Harris 15-4-59-3; Siddle 9-2-25-1; Johnson 17.3-5-38-6. *Second innings* – Hilfenhaus 10-4-16-1; Harris 11-1-47-6; Johnson 12-3-44-3; Siddle 4-1-8-0.

Umpires: B.R.Doctrove and M.Erasmus

Australia won by 267 runs

AUSTRALIA v ENGLAND
(4th Test)

At Melbourne 26-29 December 2010

AUSTRALIA

S.R.Watson c Pietersen b Tremlett	5	- lbw b Bresnan	54
P.J.Hughes c Pietersen b Bresnan	16	- run out (Trott/Prior)	23
*R.T.Ponting c Swann b Tremlett	10	- b Bresnan	20
M.J.Clarke c Prior b Anderson	20	- c Strauss b Swann	13
M.E.K.Hussey c Prior b Anderson	8	- c Bell b Bresnan	0
S.P.D.Smith c Prior b Anderson	6	- b Anderson	38
+B.J.Haddin c Strauss b Bresnan	5	- not out	55
M.G.Johnson c Prior b Anderson	0	- b Tremlett	6
R.J.Harris not out	10	- absent hurt	
P.M.Siddle c Prior b Tremlett	11	(9) c Pietersen b Swann	40
B.W.Hilfenhaus c Prior b Tremlett	0	(10) c Prior b Bresnan	0
l-b 2, n-b 5	7	B 1, l-b 6, w 2	9
	----		----
1/15 2/37 3/37 4/58	98	1/53 2/99 3/102 4/104	258
5/66 6/77 7/77 8/77 9/92 10/98		5/134 6/158 7/172 8/258 9/258	

Bowling: *First innings* – Anderson 16-4-44-4; Tremlett 11.5-5-26-4; Bresnan 13-6-25-2; Swann 2-1-1-0. *Second innings* – Anderson 20-1-71-1; Tremlett 17-3-71-1; Swann 27-11-59-2; Bresnan 21.4-8-50-4.

ENGLAND

*A.J.Strauss c Hussey b Siddle	69
A.N.Cook c Watson b Siddle	82
I.J.L.Trott not out	168
K.P.Pietersen lbw b Siddle	51
P.D.Collingwood c Siddle b Johnson	8
I.R.Bell c Siddle b Johnson	1
+M.J.Prior c Ponting b Siddle	85
T.T.Bresnan c Haddin b Siddle	4
G.P.Swann c Haddin b Hilfenhaus	22
C.T.Tremlett b Hilfenhaus	4
J.M.Anderson b Siddle	1
B 10, l-b 2, w 3, n-b 3	18

1/159 2/170 3/262 4/281	513
5/286 6/459 7/465 8/508 9/512 10/513	

Bowling: *First innings* - Hilfenhaus 37-13-83-2; Harris 28.4-9-91-0; Johnson 29-2-134-2; Siddle 33.1-10-75-6; Watson 10-1-34-0; Smith 18-3-71-0; Clarke 3.2-0-13-0.

Umpires: Aleem Dar and A.L.Hill

England won by an innings and 157 runs

AUSTRALIA v ENGLAND
(5th Test)

At Sydney 3-7 January 2011

AUSTRALIA

S.R.Watson c Strauss b Bresnan	45	- run out (Prior/Pietersen)	38
P.J.Hughes c Collingwood b Tremlett	31	- c Prior b Bresnan	13
U.T.Khawaja c Trott b Swann	37	- c Prior b Anderson	21
*M.J.Clarke c Anderson b Bresnan	4	- c Prior b Anderson	41
M.E.K.Hussey b Collingwood	33	- c Pietersen b Bresnan	12
+B.J.Haddin c Prior b Anderson	6	- c Prior b Tremlett	30
S.P.D.Smith c Collingwood b Anderson	18	- not out	54
M.G.Johnson b Bresnan	53	- b Tremlett	0
P.M.Siddle c Strauss b Anderson	2	- c Anderson b Swann	43
B.W.Hilfenhaus c Prior b Anderson	34	- c Prior b Anderson	7
M.A.Beer not out	2	- b Tremlett	2
B 5, l-b 7, w 1, n-b 2	15	B 11, l-b 4, w 3, n-b 2	20
	----		----
	280		281

1/55 2/105 3/113 4/134   280   1/46 2/52 3/117 4/124   281
5/143 6/171 7/187 8/189 9/265 10/280   5/161 6/171 7/171 8/257 9/267 10/281

Bowling: First innings - Anderson 30.1-7-66-4; Tremlett 26-9-71-1; Bresnan 30-5-89-3; Swann 16-4-37-1; Collingwood 4-2-5-1. *Second innings* – Anderson 18-5-61-3; Tremlett 20.4-4-79-3; Swann 28-8-75-1; Bresnan 18-6-51-2.

ENGLAND

*A.J.Strauss b Hilfenhaus	60
A.N.Cook c Hussey b Watson	189
I.J.L.Trott b Johnson	0
K.P.Pietersen c Beer b Johnson	36
J.M.Anderson b Siddle	7
P.D.Collingwood c Hilfenhaus b Beer	13
I.R.Bell c Clarke b Johnson	115
+M.J.Prior c Haddin b Hilfenhaus	118
T.T.Bresnan c Clarke b Johnson	35
G.P.Swann not out	36
C.T.Tremlett c Haddin b Hilfenhaus	12
B 3, l-b 11, w 5, n-b 4	23

	644

1/98 2/99 3/165 4/181   644
5/226 6/380 7/487 8/589 9/609 10/644

Bowling: First innings - Hilfenhaus 38.5-7-121-3; Johnson 36-5-168-4; Siddle 31-5-111-1; Watson 20-7-49-1; Beer 38-3-112-1; Smith 13-0-67-0; Hussey 1-0-2-0.

Umpires: Aleem Dar and B.F.Bowden

England won by an innings and 83 runs

THE ASHES 2010–11 PLAYER AVERAGES

Compiled by Victor Isaacs

AUSTRALIA

Batting averages

Player	Mat	Inns	NO	Runs	HS	Avge	SR	100	50	Ct	St
M.E.K. Hussey	5	9	0	570	195	63.33	52.53	2	3	5	-
S.R. Watson	5	10	1	435	95	48.33	48.17	-	4	5	-
B.J. Haddin	5	9	1	360	136	45.00	54.87	1	3	8	1
S.P.D. Smith	3	6	1	159	54*	31.80	49.07	-	1	2	-
U.T. Khawaja	1	2	0	58	37	29.00	34.52	-	-	-	-
S.M. Katich	2	4	0	97	50	24.25	46.85	-	1	1	-
M.J. Clarke	5	9	0	193	80	21.44	44.16	-	1	3	-
P.M. Siddle	5	9	1	154	43	19.25	56.41	-	-	2	-
M.G. Johnson	4	7	0	122	62	17.42	58.37	-	2	-	-
M.J. North	2	3	0	49	26	16.33	36.02	-	-	1	-
P.J. Hughes	3	6	0	97	31	16.16	38.80	-	-	-	-
R.T. Ponting	4	8	1	113	51*	16.14	51.59	-	1	4	-
B.W. Hilfenhaus	4	7	2	55	34	11.00	50.92	-	-	1	-
X.J. Doherty	2	3	0	27	16	9.00	46.55	-	-	-	-
M.A. Beer	1	2	1	4	2*	4.00	15.38	-	-	1	-
R.J. Harris	3	5	1	14	10*	3.50	37.83	-	-	-	-
D.E. Bollinger	1	2	2	7	7*	-	36.84	-	-	-	-

Bowling averages

Player	Overs	Mdns	Runs	Wkts	Avge	Econ	SR	BBI	BBM	5wI	10wM
R.J. Harris	83.4	19	281	11	25.54	3.35	45.6	6/47	9/106	1	-
P.M. Siddle	147.1	28	484	14	34.57	3.28	63.0	6/54	6/75	2	-
M.G. Johnson	136.3	22	554	15	36.93	4.05	54.6	6/38	9/82	1	-
B.W. Hilfenhaus	157.5	42	415	7	59.28	2.62	135.2	3/121	3/121	-	-
S.R. Watson	76.0	19	223	3	74.33	2.93	152.0	1/30	1/44	-	-
X.J. Doherty	75.5	11	306	3	102.00	4.03	151.6	2/41	2/148	-	-
M.J. North	38.0	3	110	1	110.00	2.89	228.0	1/47	1/48	-	-
M.A. Beer	38.0	3	112	1	112.00	2.94	228.0	1/112	1/112	-	-
D.E. Bollinger	29.0	1	130	1	130.00	4.48	174.0	1/130	1/130	-	-
S.P.D. Smith	31.0	3	138	0	-	4.45	-	-	-	-	-
M.J. Clarke	3.2	0	13	0	-	3.90	-	-	-	-	-
M.E.K. Hussey	1.0	0	2	0	-	2.00	-	-	-	-	-

ENGLAND

Batting averages

Player	Mat	Inns	NO	Runs	HS	Avge	SR	100	50	Ct	St
A.N. Cook	5	7	1	766	235*	127.66	53.26	3	2	5	-
I.J.L. Trott	5	7	2	445	168*	89.00	50.39	2	1	1	-
I.R. Bell	5	6	1	329	115	65.80	56.14	1	3	3	-
K.P. Pietersen	5	6	0	360	227	60.00	63.94	1	1	5	-
M.J. Prior	5	6	1	252	118	50.40	78.26	1	1	23	-
A.J. Strauss	5	7	0	307	110	43.85	51.85	1	3	8	-
G.P. Swann	5	5	1	88	36*	22.00	88.88	-	-	6	-
T.T. Bresnan	2	2	0	39	35	19.50	32.50	-	-	-	-
P.D. Collingwood	5	6	0	83	42	13.83	46.62	-	-	9	-
C.T. Tremlett	3	4	1	19	12	6.33	36.53	-	-	-	-
J.M. Anderson	5	5	0	22	11	4.40	26.50	-	-	4	-
S.T. Finn	3	3	0	3	2	3.00	37.50	-	-	2	-
S.C. J.Broad	2	1	0	0	0	0.00	0.00	-	-	-	-

Bowling averages

Player	Overs	Mdns	Runs	Wkts	Avge	Econ	SR	BBI	BBM	5wI	10wM
T.T. Bresnan	82.4	25	215	11	19.54	2.60	45.0	4/50	6/75	1	-
C.T. Tremlett	122.3	28	397	17	23.35	3.24	43.2	5/87	8/150	1	-
J.M. Anderson	213.1	50	625	24	26.04	2.93	53.2	4/44	7/127	-	-
S.T. Finn	107.4	9	464	14	33.14	4.30	46.1	6/125	6/150	1	-
G.P. Swann	219.1	43	597	15	39.80	2.72	87.6	5/91	7/161	1	-
K.P. Pietersen	5.0	0	16	1	16.00	3.20	30.0	1/10	1/10	-	-
P.D. Collingwood	31.0	6	73	2	36.50	2.35	93.0	1/3	1/5	-	-
S.C. J.Broad	69.5	17	161	2	80.50	2.30	209.5	1/18	1/71	-	-

INDEX

INDEX

INDEX